Ultimate High

Ultimate High

My Everest Odyssey

Göran Kropp

with David Lagercrantz

DISCOVERY BOOKS
New York

Text copyright © 1997 by Göran Kropp and David Lagercrantz

All rights reserved under International and Pan-American
Copyright Conventions. Published in the United States in 1999 by
Discovery Books, an imprint of Random House, Inc., New York,
and simultaneously in Canada by Random House of Canada
Limited, Toronto.

Originally published in Sweden in 1997 by Bokförlaget DN

English translation copyright © 1999 by Ola Klingberg

Discovery Communications, Inc., produces high-quality television
programming, interactive media, books, films, and consumer
products. Discovery Networks, a division of Discovery
Communications, Inc., operates and manages the Discovery
Channel, TLC, Animal Planet, and Travel Channel.

DISCOVERY BOOKS and the Discovery Books colophon are registered
trademarks of Discovery Communications, Inc.

Library of Congress Cataloging-in-Publication Data
Kropp, Göran.
    [Göran Kropp. English]
    Ultimate high: my everest odyssey / Göran Kropp with
David Lagercrantz.
        p.   cm.
    ISBN 1-56331-830-X (hardcover)
    1. Kropp, Göran.   2. Mountaineers — Sweden Biography.
3. Mountaineering — Everest, Mount (China and Nepal)
4. Everest, Mount (China and Nepal) — Description and travel.
I. Lagercrantz, David.   II. Title.
    GV199.92.K76 A313   1999   796.52'2'092 — dc21   99-32510
                                    [B]

Random House website address: www.atrandom.com

Discovery Communications website address: www.discovery.com

Printed in the United States of America on acid-free paper

10 9 8 7 6 5 4 3 2 1

First U.S. Edition

Book design by Michael Hentges
Maps by Magnus Nilsson

To Mats and the others
who didn't return

Prologue

THE SHERPAS ON OUR EXPEDITION ARE WORRIED. The eerie smudge of the comet Hyakutake in the night sky alarms them. The comet is a cosmic apparition, but they think that it is a sign of wrongdoing and a dangerous portent. What troubles them deeply is actually something very serious. Things have changed on Mount Everest in recent years, and much for the worse, they believe. To the Sherpas, Everest—or in their language, Chomolungma, the Goddess Mother of the World—is not just any mountain, a summit to be climbed and collected and added to a list of accomplishments.

"Everest is no mountain. Everest is God. Everest is God for all Sherpas here," the legendary Sherpa Ang Rita tells me, and he means it.

The most important thing, he explains, is not to anger the mountain. You must first learn the rituals and rules that Everest demands and deserves. Climbers must revere the mountain as they would their own god.

"On the living shell of Everest—on its divine body—you have to act in a decent manner," Ang Rita says. "If not, the holy wrath of the mountain may strike us all, and that wrath is as powerful as the Flood of the Christian god."

On May 10, 1996, I watch from Base Camp as dark clouds drift across and obscure the summits of nearby Pumori and Nuptse. In late afternoon, the storm hits Mount Everest, striking it with shocking violence. Now, howling across the mountain's upper slopes without mercy, the blizzard rages. We are told that the New Zealand mountain guide Rob Hall—the most well-respected climber on the mountain—has been trapped by the storm at 28,800 feet. Less than 300 feet below Everest's summit, Rob is waiting to die.

Huddled with fellow climbers in a supply tent in Base Camp, I listen in and follow the changes in Rob's mood over the radio. At first he sounds groggy, but later, after he finds a couple of oxygen bottles at the South Summit and can breathe from them, Rob observes in a matter-of-fact voice that his hands have been destroyed by frostbite.

"Just send up a couple of guys with a big thermos of something hot, then I'll be fine," he says on the radio.

The capacity for irony seems to be the last thing that deserts a dying man.

Several hundred yards lower down the mountain, the American guide Scott Fischer and Taiwanese climber Makalu Gau are sitting together. Although they are members of separate expeditions, we learn that for some reason they are now roped to each other. We can't figure out how they ended up together. While Makalu Gau is considered something of a greenhorn, Scott has a worldwide reputation. He's a guy who radiates charm—and enthusiasm and skill. Although we surmise Scott is frostbitten and his supply of bottled oxygen has run out, we do not know that he has also already lost his mind. I know it sounds horrible to say this, because Scott Fischer is my friend. But even experienced climbers go mad from anoxia, the lack of oxygen. And when madness happens, the end is often near.

"I'm going to jump down," Scott Fischer states over and over again into his radio, and we know he won't live much longer.

On the subzero wasteland of Everest's South Col, the physician Seaborn Beck Weathers has also been trapped in the storm and incapacitated by anoxia after his bottled oxygen ran out. Left by his companions to die, Weathers lies corpse-like with his right hand exposed to the bitter cold. Yet the will to live is indomitable; a little later, Weathers musters himself to stand up, as if rising from the dead. His arm is outstretched, frozen into an insane half-bent gesture. Looking at it, Weathers wonders if it's really his arm and his hand. It no longer looks like a part of his body.

Back down at 17,100 feet, Base Camp—which only a little while ago was like a vacation resort—is in chaos. Over the radio, we hear that twenty people are dead up on the mountain. Then the figure drops to ten, and a moment later to one, before almost predictably it begins to rise again. Meanwhile, we are doing what we can to help. We ask our Sherpas Kami and Ang Rita to climb up with medicine. They refuse.

The mountain is angry, they say.

Everest is taking its revenge on the climbers, they tell us, for their vain pride and for fornicating on the divine flanks of the mountain. When Kami and Ang Rita refuse, I decide to go with the medicine myself. But my girlfriend, Renata, objects.

"What good will it do if you die, too?" she shouts at me.

Renata knows all too well that I am totally exhausted. I have already made the first summit attempt of the season, but I was defeated. Just four days ago, I managed to descend back to Base Camp, staggering to the tents in a drug-like stupor, my lips blue-black, and gazing with vacant eyes straight up into the sky.

"I've given all I have," I told Renata, and I wept.

As I'd headed for Everest's summit, I struggled uphill through deep snow at 28,670 feet—not far from where Rob Hall was now stuck. But I realized that it was too late in the day; I knew

I couldn't reach the top and still return before dark, so I turned around. I had no choice. If I wanted to live, I had to turn back. The decision was simple, but I had given the summit my all. The effort had emptied me.

On my descent, I pushed my body far beyond the point of complete exhaustion. I no longer cared if I lived or died. As I entered Base Camp, both of my legs buckled out from under me. I had lost an incredible amount of weight, and my body was crying out for fat and nourishment. Before I sank into a deep sleep, I devoured a whole can of butter; my wasted muscles demanded it. The next morning, I doubted I could regain my strength for another summit try. Now all the other climbers are heading for the top, everybody but me. I've been left behind, and I feel gnawing pangs of envy. Why, I wonder, hadn't I been able to summit on my first attempt? What had I done wrong?

Then the storm comes. More complicated and traumatic feelings overwhelm me. Now several of the people I have come to know and love are dying on the mountain. Sitting alone in the snow, they listen to the howling gale. All afternoon, I pace back and forth in Base Camp and look at the sky. Soon darkness and a vast loneliness will descend upon the mountain; it will be a black night, without stars. At 6:15 P.M., I return to the square supply tent. Twenty-five people are inside. They sit on narrow, plastic-covered mattresses. I can see the faces of only those closest to the tent opening, where there is a table with a satellite telephone, a fax machine, and a kerosene lamp, which spreads a faint light. The others are rendered into silhouettes by the lantern's feeble glow. The tent walls are dark green. People speak in whispers.

"Göran," somebody says. "Perhaps you can guide Rob back down over the radio. You've been up there."

I know that's not possible, but I say, "Sure, of course." The fact that Rob Hall is still alive is amazing enough, but many hours have passed since the storm's onset, and few people have any illusions left that he will survive. Right then, Jan Arnold, Rob's wife, calls from New Zealand. She wants to talk to her husband. The call is patched through to Rob.

"Give me a minute," he says, in a cracked and dry voice. "I want to eat a bit of snow before I talk to her."

Then the radio falls silent. People fidget and put their arms around each other. For a moment I feel uncomfortable, as if this were a memorial service to which I was not really invited. Then we hear Jan's voice. The radio crackles; she says something.

"I hope you're tucked up in a nice warm bed," Rob answers.

"I can't tell you how much I'm thinking about you," I remember her saying.

"Sleep well, my sweetheart. Please don't worry too much."

"See you," she says, wishing.

The people inside the tent edge closer to each other on the mattresses. Someone utters a curse, and wet eyes gleam in the darkness. Then silence returns until two men cautiously start discussing the conversation. I pick up the radio, and one of the women at the table nods gravely at me. I call, as agreed: "Rob Hall. Over!"

I hear a crackling noise. The radio seems to be searching through various frequencies, but there is no sound from Rob, nothing. Instead I get another voice.

"He's probably too tired to talk to you," the voice says.

I go outside. There are perhaps a hundred tents pitched on the moraines of the Khumbu Glacier. Inside some of them, generators buzz in the dusk, while the glacial ice moves and makes cracking sounds and the prayer-flags strung on long strings flap in the slight wind. Nearby, some incense is burning. But the white mountains that encircle the camp—the peaks we have all come here to climb—have faded into the darkness. Into this long night of death.

"Hell!" I think. "Why should this happen?"

I hardly dare acknowledge my next thought. It is selfish, but I think it anyway. Does this tragedy on Everest mean that the greatest project of my life is ruined? Will I have to return home now without reaching the summit after years of preparation and effort?

Or, somehow, can I climb in the footsteps of the dead? In the tracks of my friends who are dying tonight? What will people think of me if I do? Do I still have enough strength to climb Everest without bottled oxygen and without Sherpas? And will the weather improve again before the summer monsoon rains come?

Those were my thoughts on the evening of the eleventh of May, 1996.

Ultimate High

1

W HAT'S DRIVING YOU, I AM
often asked. A death wish?

I do not want to die, certainly not yet.

"A zest for life," I answer. Mountaineering gives me the most
beautiful things in life: encounters with other cultures, natural
beauty, challenges, triumphs.

My climbing interest started early, in Italy where my family
lived when I was a kid. My father, Gerard, was a lawyer for the UN
agency FAO. Dad went climbing in the Italian Dolomites, and I
watched him from the foot of the mountain through my binocu-
lars. Sometimes when I looked at his equipment, his hammer,
carabiners, and ropes, I sensed a certain solemn feeling.

People have told me that the first words I uttered were
"climb mountain," and at the age of six, I went hiking with Dad to
the top of Galdhøppigen, the highest peak in Norway. A year later,
we went to the top of Kebnekaise, Sweden's tallest peak. Those
were big events for a small boy. Still, my passion for climbing
developed only slowly, and when I reached my teens, I forgot all
about the mountains. My parents split up in 1976, and for a long

time, I lived with my mother, Sigrun, outside Stockholm. I have no sisters or brothers. My mother, a nurse, and I got along well, although our relationship was not entirely devoid of conflict. I played flute in the municipal music school and also belonged to a local band that sometimes paraded through the city.

I was a school champion in cross-country skiing. In my studies, I was especially good at math. I was considered well behaved, but perhaps the most unusual thing about me was that I disliked team sports. I've never fully understood this feeling, but I knew quite early that I wanted to challenge myself and compete, but alone. And also, I wanted to be outside; I missed being in nature. After my parents' divorce, I didn't get to hike much. My father picked up on this. He wanted me to come live with him, and every time we talked, he tempted me with promises of the great outdoors. I was fifteen and restless; finally I packed my bags and left our Stockholm suburb and moved to my father's home. Dad had become manager of the legal department of the National Board of Forestry, located in the town of Jönköping in southern Sweden.

After the divorce, my father had turned into something of a bachelor. He was no longer used to sharing a home, and as for myself, I was on my way to becoming an adult. We collided – a little. This was in the early 1980s, and the punk-rock movement was already well established. There was a clear decadent vein in rock music at that time, but there were also links going back to the progressive movement of the '70s. The Swedish punk-rock band Ebba Grön was a new star in the sky of rock, and at an outdoor venue in Stockholm, a new audience record was set when Bob Marley performed. A year later he died. I did not remain unaffected by his death.

I started high school in Jönköping, and during my first year, I took school pretty seriously. But as time went by, school felt more and more meaningless. I switched to another study program, an easier one, which was also one year shorter. I let my hair grow long.

Soon it reached below my shoulders. I wore patched jeans and Rasta-colored skateboard shoes. My father didn't like it. We fought about chores and homework. Finally, when I was sixteen, I moved to a place of my own. I paid the rent by delivering papers. At 3:00 or 4:00 A.M., I forced myself to get up, then I put the local papers in people's mailboxes. When I got back home, I collapsed in bed. Often I didn't make it to school until the afternoon. My attendance was reported as "nonmeasurable."

In my 330-square-foot pad, I had a television and a bed; that was just about it. I put up a poster of Bob Marley on the wall, and I painted the cabinet doors in the kitchen in the Rasta colors. I partied a lot, and in school I received a warning according to the 9th chapter, 57th paragraph of the School Ordinance. "According to concordant witnesses," the warning read, "Göran Kropp has acted in an unsuitable manner toward the women in the class." Perhaps there was some truth in it; I was restless and unruly. Still, I think my improper behavior was mostly a figment of my teacher's imagination. She was very religious and tended to overreact to anything that threatened order in her class. She definitely didn't like me; I had too many wild ideas.

One day we went on an educational visit to a court of appeal. I sat at the back of the courtroom with a friend of mine. We were bored. This DUI case didn't resemble the court cases we'd seen in American movies one bit. We left. Coming out from the courtroom, we noticed a key sitting in the lock in the oak doors. We looked at each other, turned the key, pulled it out, and left.

The next day, the local paper wrote: "The court got a taste of its own medicine—locked up for six hours."

They had to call a locksmith to open the door. Witnesses had seen two young suspects leave the court laughing. We were a bit shaken. We cleaned off the key with gasoline to erase all fingerprints and returned it in an anonymous letter.

Parties were plentiful; so were rock concerts. I went to festivals both in Sweden and in Denmark. During one trip, my friends ended up in either police cells or brothels. At a concert, I jumped up on stage with Joakim Thåström of the rock band Imperiet and shouted, "The government is capitalist!" Thåström was my hero. He signed my shoe. I saw him again many times.

Emma Sjöberg, the future Swedish supermodel, and her sister, Anna-Karin, were both in my class. Anna-Karin called me Body, referring to the meaning of my last name in Swedish — Kropp means body.

"Body," she said. "We're going to an Eva Dahlgren concert in Gislaved. Why don't you come along?"

Eva Dahlgren, who is now arguably the most accomplished pop and rock singer in Sweden, was still very young then. I didn't know much about her. But it sounded like fun, so we drove through the forest in a small VW Golf until we reached the little town of Gislaved with its outdoor venue. There was a lot of confusion trying to get into the concert. People were shouting and swaying, and there was a long line to the ticket booth.

It was late spring or early summer before school was out, and it wasn't dark yet. As I stood in the throng, I decided just to crash the thing. I got down on my hands and knees and crawled past the line. No one seemed to get angry; no one even looked surprised. I guess I wasn't the only one crawling around that night. I don't remember much of the concert. The audience consisted mainly of young girls, and Eva Dahlgren sang songs I had never heard before. But afterward — I won't ever forget this — Anna-Karin came up to me. She looked embarrassed.

"Sorry, Body," she said. "The car is full. You have to get home on your own."

That was a shock. I didn't have any money — I didn't have anything. But after strolling around for a while, thinking the situation through, I went backstage, where I saw Eva Dahlgren, the rising blond star. She was dressed in black pants and a white tank top and sat surrounded by her fans, signing autographs but looking a bit lost. Behind her stood a long line of shy teenage girls.

"Hi," I said, when all the fans had gone. "I have a problem. I need a ride."

Eva Dahlgren looked at me, and there I stood with long unkempt hair, ripped jeans, and a Bob Marley T-shirt. I think we hit it off somehow.

"Sure," she said. "Come on." I got a lift in her bus, but I noticed that one of her musicians, the producer Anders Glenmark, was annoyed. "What is that little brat doing in our bus?" he seemed to be thinking—and I couldn't help but wonder the same thing. I didn't care, though, because Eva Dahlgren was an angel. She got me a hotel room in the next town on their tour, and we drank and had fun together, and I think I fell in love. Nothing happened, I'm sad to say. Perhaps I was just a funny diversion to her, but still she asked me to join them in Oslo, Norway. Sadly, I had to say no. I had to go back home; my absences from school were mounting.

Now, over a decade later, I sometimes look back at those years and I don't regret anything. I'm glad I had all of those experiences. Although I didn't party for a very long period, I did party very hard. Now when I look back at those days, I wonder why I did it. Perhaps I needed to break free, to make a new life for myself away from Gerard, my dad. Nowadays, we are better friends than ever, but in my teenage years I was restless and I wanted things to happen. And, ironically, I couldn't find what I was looking for in my father's life interest: the great outdoors and nature. I found my life in partying and in music.

At a concert in another small town, I played saxophone with a little-known band, Telephåne. Later, someone stole my saxophone, but my love for music never went away. I still have it, and at critical moments up in the mountains, I listen to soul music to recharge myself and to survive, and sometimes when people I've known have died climbing, I've channeled my grief by listening to music. After the Mount Everest tragedy in the spring of 1996, I played Bach's "Air" on my flute at our stupa in Base Camp, the blessing altar where we gathered to pray to the mountain gods. It was soothing, like a ritual—a gesture of reverence to the mountain and to those who never came back.

During my last year in high school, my wild period ended. I stopped partying. I wanted more out of life. Or maybe I just switched from one extreme to another. I decided I wanted to be a paratrooper. I was about to be called up for my mandatory national service, and I decided that either I would go for the easiest, most unqualified position there was—or I would go for the toughest. So without anything dramatic happening, one day I started lifting weights. And every day I ran six miles. Later that fall, I was accepted as a paratrooper.

In the barracks, I met a guy who read mountaineering magazines. His name was Mats Dahlin. He was a fair-skinned boy with a crew cut. Although he was taciturn and considered a bit strange, we hit it off, and Mats's love of the mountains rekindled my own childhood interest in climbing. Memories of my early outdoor adventures came rushing back like a surging river. I began reading about the great mountains and the people who first scaled them— and about the discipline that is required if you want to survive on the world's highest peaks. I read about Reinhold Messner, the greatest climber of them all. Often Messner ran up a 3,600-vertical-foot hill near his home in Italy. His wife waited for him in their car at the summit. She drove him back down, then he ran back up—again and again and again. It came as a realization to me, seeing how hard Messner trained. One day, I sent Mats a postcard that said:

"I want to get up above 8,000 meters. Will you join me?"

And he answered: "Toward 8,000!"

Mats and I made a pact to go climbing together, and we started training hard. Sometimes we set out on an infernal mountain march from the northern Swedish town of Abisko in Lapland to the neighboring village of Nikkaluokta—65 miles. We called it the Willpower March, because that's what it was all about. Having the will to succeed. We carried backpacks so heavy that we had a hard time even picking them up; we pressed ourselves to the pain threshold and beyond. We were obsessed, and I had changed.

How did the reggae guy become a mountaineer? I can't explain it—at least not to people who have never experienced the magic lure and ancient power of the mountains, those who have never dreamed of trekking through an unknown land, and who are not, when seeing a picture of a beautiful mountain, filled with reverence and a sudden longing. But I can tell you about my drive and motivation purely as an athlete. Mats and I wanted to become the stars of our sport. We wanted to do what no one had done before. Our dreams were not about becoming world champions in soccer or marathon running; our dreams were of the Himalaya.

Mountaineering, we also soon learned, was very expensive. The equipment cost money. The expeditions, the porters to carry supplies, and the government climbing permits cost even more. For a long time I didn't know how to support myself. I enjoyed being a paratrooper when I did my military service, and I believed that a career as an officer would give me opportunities to train. I got a job at an infantry regiment in the little town of Eksjö in southern Sweden. The pay was horrible: about $12,000 a year before taxes. I realized that I had to choose between paying rent— and going climbing. The choice was simple. One summer I gave up my apartment and moved to a military training area a quarter mile from the barracks. I lived alone in my two-man tent close to a running track. It was all right for a while, but one night, a group of soldiers on guard duty stumbled over one of my tent ropes.

"Investigate!" I heard the one in charge call out.

"Stop!" I shouted. "It's Second Lieutenant Kropp living here!"

After that incident, I decided to move farther away, to a gravel pit. I lived there for a year. In the daytime, I was a military cadet. In the evenings, I worked out with weights or ran for three hours. Then I would walk the four miles "home" to my gravel pit, a lonely place no one ever visited—except for two policemen who arrived one morning and demanded to know who I was.

"Only me," I answered. "Cadet Kropp."

Earlier, to practice my rock climbing skills, I had scaled the outside of the old stone water tower in Eksjö. It was over a hundred feet tall. The very next day after the policemen investigated my campsite—almost as if to underscore how crazy I was—the local paper published a story about me climbing the water tower. I still wonder what the policemen must have thought when they read that article at their breakfast tables.

"Hey, look—there he is. The crazy guy from the gravel pit!"

Autumn came. I moved again and camped next to my old, worn-out BMW. I strung an electrical cord from the cigarette lighter into the tent so I could plug in my tape recorder. I loved to listen to James Brown, the Pretenders, and Bob Marley. My other possessions were a sleeping bag, a lamp, some clothing, a few books about climbing—and my alarm clock.

As an experiment, I began to set the alarm to go off at night at a random hour. If it went off at 3:00 A.M., I got up, dressed quickly, and walked for thirty kilometers (nineteen miles) with a light backpack. If it went off at six, I marched fast for sixty kilometers (thirty-seven miles). I continued to think about Messner, and I wondered if I could climb like him. Did I have enough willpower yet? In those frugal and spartan years, that's what kept me going: the dream of climbing.

I knew from my reading what high-altitude climbing was like. At an altitude of 26,000 feet, at night it's minus twenty degrees Fahrenheit outside. You lie in your tent, it's hard even to breathe, and you feel groggy and slow, as if you were wading through water, but still, you have to get up before dawn and head for the summit. On a big climb, I didn't want to be the one to have to drop out. So I was obsessive about training.

At this point in my life, in 1988, I had attended a climbing course with the Swedish Climbing Association in the Dolomites. I had scaled mountains in Corsica, and Mats and I ascended Mont Blanc in the Alps. But still I lacked climbing experience above 20,000 feet. To remedy this, next Mats and I chose 23,406-foot Pik Lenin in Kyrgyzstan. It's one of the easiest peaks of that altitude in the world, and many mountaineers pick it for their first high-altitude climb.

Before we left home, we were pretty nervous, wondering how we would cope with the thin air. Different people have different reactions to high altitude. Many climbers get queasy stomachs, feel nauseous, or become apathetic. Others suffer acute headaches. The lack of oxygen also greatly diminishes a person's powers of reason and judgment. Most serious, however, is when body liquid separates from the blood and gathers either in the lungs or between the brain and the skull. These high-altitude illnesses, respectively called pulmonary edema and cerebral edema, often lead to death.

Mats and I had memorized the warning signs; we knew the dangers. On Pik Lenin we might be struck down by high-altitude illness and discover the sad truth that we were not cut out for the goal to which we had devoted our lives.

We had worked hard to prepare ourselves for the climb, and we wanted to show it. We scaled Pik Lenin faster than anyone ever had. In fact, the ascent was almost an anticlimax. Lenin's summit is large and rounded and not at all distinct. We wandered around up there for some time, searching for the famous communist-era plaque of Lenin that marks the top. After a while we noticed some other climbers staring at something, but they were below us! So we descended for a quick visit with Lenin. I thought I'd had it so easy, but once we headed down toward Base Camp, I started throwing up. My head was pounding, and every step felt unreal. I felt like I was traveling through a vacuum, moving in slow motion.

"I'm at 23,000 feet, and I can't possibly feel any worse. How will I ever be able to get higher?" I remember thinking.

What I didn't realize then was that my body was getting acclimatized, or acclimated, to the lack of oxygen, and that next time I went high, I would feel a lot better. Even today after numerous ascents to extreme altitudes, I still experience a feeling up there that I can't quite describe. It's been said that a physically fit person becomes like a seventy-year-old at 7,000 meters (23,000 feet) above sea level, and like an eighty-year-old at 8,000 meters (26,000 feet). For lack of a better comparison, I sometimes compare these lethargic, disembodied sensations to being drunk. But on a mountain, even though your body is groggy and clumsy, you must stay in absolute control and act soberly. The good thing about climbing (unlike drinking) is that afterward the joy stays with you while the pain goes away.

Following our success on Lenin, Mats and I laughed at our ailments and decided that our next mountain should be above 8,000 meters — one of the famous "8,000-ers." We picked Cho Oyu, the eighth-tallest mountain in the world, which was first scaled by the Austrian Herbert Tichy in 1954. The '50s were a glorious decade in mountaineering, when all of the world's fourteen peaks above 8,000 meters were first conquered (at least all but number thirteen on the list, Shisha Pangma). Cho Oyu is situated on the border between Nepal and Chinese-occupied Tibet, and sadly we now experienced yet another reality of high-altitude mountaineering. The political situation and ongoing border problems with regard to Tibetan refugees made it impossible for us to obtain permission to attempt Cho Oyu.

So instead, in 1989 I went climbing by myself in the Andes of South America. And on this expedition I learned much more about the joys and sufferings of mountaineers. Mist, steam, and the stinging smell of sulfur greeted me on the crater rim summit of Cotopaxi in Ecuador, the tallest active volcano in the world. Then, on nearby Chimborazo, an earthquake tore loose the frozen snowfield I was climbing. In desperation to save myself, I ran on top of the sliding floe, riding this giant natural surfboard out of control as it slid down the mountainside, thinking my time had come. Luckily, I stopped fifty feet from a precipice – but that is another story.

After I scaled one last volcano, Illampu, from the summit I chose another, even faster, method of descent – but one I had more control over: by hang glider. In only eight minutes, I flew from the roughly 20,000-foot-elevation summit all the way down to our 13,000-foot Base Camp. I was screaming with joy as I sailed past mountain tops peeking through the carpet of clouds beneath me. And this time I landed on level ground, not next to a cliff face! My French companions eventually rejoined me, but they bolted straight over a mountain pass to the closest village.

I'd been feeling sick with bouts of fever on and off for several weeks, but each time I'd gotten well again. Now my illness chose a poor time to return. Typhoid fever is like that; it comes and goes. In any case, I was too weak to join the Frenchmen, so I staggered downhill, alone now, to a mountain road. Even though the terrain wasn't difficult, I began to stumble; soon I collapsed. Goats and llamas grazed on the hillsides. Fortunately I found a small stream by the roadside, unfurled my sleeping bag next to it, and crawled inside, waiting for help to come. For someone to give me a lift to the nearest town.

Then the fever came on. And the diarrhea. I was too weak to pull myself out of my sleeping bag, so now things had gotten considerably worse. The smell! It was a strange and awful night, and my eyes wouldn't even focus on the stars. In the morning, I had lost so much fluid and was so dehydrated that I forced myself to crawl to the brook and drank and drank. I was groggy, but I still thought: "Sooner or later, a car will come by and take me to the village." But no cars drove by. And that day passed. Then a new day came and passed. Still no cars.

On the afternoon of the third day, a shabby red pickup carrying a load of slaughtered animals came along, headed in the wrong direction. I didn't care where I went as long as it was closer to civilization. The driver helped me up, and I sat amongst dead beasts, suffering from stomach illness and nausea. I mumbled to myself: "It's all right now. I will get help."

But I soon realized how little a human life is worth to some people. I was dumped in a godforsaken farming village called Ancohuma, four miles from where I wanted to go. I sat in my soiled sleeping bag in the middle of the town square behind a stone wall and some clay huts; I could no longer stand up. When I asked to be driven to the hospital in Sorata, the passersby just smiled.

"Gringo," people said, laughing when I tried to stand and collapsed.

For six days, I lay in the village square, drinking only water. I ate no food. Finally, a teacher came, brought me home with him, and gave me an orange, the first thing I'd eaten in nine days. That night I suffered an epileptic-like seizure. Then I felt two men lift me. The people finally understood: The gringo was dying. For thirty dollars, they gave me a ride to Sorata.

When I arrived at the town hospital, a nurse saw me and laughed. She must have thought my misery was comical, and in a way, I fully understood her. I crept through the hospital hallway, pushing my backpack in front of me. I was put in a room where the beds were so small that they had to put three of them next to each other and lay me down across them. My roommate's name was King Lee.

"I'm Bruce Lee's brother," he claimed, which I doubted. "I run the gold mining up here." That I did not doubt. There were gold mines in these mountains. A sign of Lee's importance stood outside of our door: an armed bodyguard cradling a Kalashnikov. Then King Lee fingered the loaded Magnum pistol sitting on his bedside table. King Lee was one macho fellow.

"You cannot turn off the light. You must leave it on," he said. "We have to watch out."

For whom, I barely dared think. So there we lay, all night long, King Lee and I, with the lamps turned on.

"I have to get out of here," I thought. I persuaded the staff to drive me to the capital, La Paz, for $100. Vaguely I remember being dumped on a sidewalk, but then through a lucky quirk of fate, a guy from the small Swedish town of Alingsås walked by, and he took me to a miserable hotel that charged only a dollar a night.

While I lay tossing and turning in my hotel bed, I heard a familiar voice in the hallway.

"It can't be true," I mumbled. "I'm delirious. It's the fever."

But it really did sound like Gabi Bavli, the craziest guy I know. I'd met him on a climbing course in the Dolomites. I staggered to the door, opened it with shaking hands—and there he was. Gabi looked at me as if he'd seen a ghost.

"Göran!" he said. "What on earth has happened to you?"

"Gabi, I'm very sick."

"I can see that. But we have to celebrate! You're here, and I can't believe it!" Then suddenly Gabi stared at me as if he understood what bad shape I was in. Then he disappeared, for help, I hoped.

I went back to bed. I drifted in and out of strange dreams;

time passed. An hour? Twelve hours? The sweat-soaked sheets clung to my skin; the outlines of the grayish room blurred. The air in the room was stagnant and still. When someone knocked on the door, I didn't know where I was. I raised my head with difficulty. Gabi entered the room with two giggling women who looked at me, evidently amused, as if I were on exhibit.

"You're hopeless," I told Gabi. Then my head hit the pillow. Two days later, in a hospital in Lima, Peru, I was so dehydrated the doctors had to stick the IV needle between my knuckles. I didn't get well until nine weeks later at an infection clinic in Stockholm.

I suppose some climbers might have been put off by the awful experiences that I had in South America. Once I recovered, though, I was still keen on going on another expedition. I guess I really am a hard case! The next year, I wanted to try the Muztagh Tower in Pakistan, 23,917 feet tall—and known as the Impossible Mountain. Only four people had ever scaled it, and when I saw a picture, I understood why. Smooth, vertical rock walls guarded every flank. Muztagh Tower would require steep climbing at high altitude. It looked like a mountain you ought to leave alone, this impregnable peak, but we went anyway: Ola Hillberg, Magnus Nilsson, Erik Ringius, Anders Rafael Jensen, Anders Nygren, and I.

Before every expedition, you must discuss and calculate how much food and equipment you will need, and how many porters must be hired to carry it all. On Muztagh we needed sixty-two porters, even though the porters' food walked on its own legs: a herd of goats, which were slaughtered one by one on the approach.

"The animals don't feel anything," said the Muslim who performed the job. He took out his hopelessly blunt knife and virtually sawed off the neck of a goat that let out heartrending shrieks as he did so. Killing animals was unusual cruelty, I decided, and I became a vegetarian.

Later I also grew increasingly disenchanted with the whole industry of using porters on mountaineering expeditions. There was no dignity in it for these men, I thought—just danger and a miserable salary. The more Balti porters (the Pakistani equivalent of Sherpas) that we needed to carry our food and equipment, the more unnecessary trash was created. It was this feeling of unnecessary logistics and wastefulness, I think, that became the kernel of my Everest-by-bicycle climb, my solo expedition where I carried everything that I needed to Base Camp by myself.

On Muztagh Tower, snow bridges collapsed under us, we dodged falling stones, and when a rope unexpectedly broke, Magnus Nilsson nearly plummeted 4,000 feet down the South Face. The climb's final stretch ascended a steep, infernal wall. We belayed ourselves with ropes while we struggled up, panting heavily in the thin air. We concentrated on only the section in front of us. We'd been staring into the ice and rocks for such a long time that when I reached the summit plateau and pulled myself up in amazement, it was as if a curtain had been pulled away. The fear fled, and the mountain wall was replaced by a vision of paradise.

In my euphoric dizziness, I could see Broad Peak and the whole range of the Karakoram mountains through the crystal-clear air; and then, unannounced, I saw for the first time K2, perhaps the world's most beautiful mountain. K2 cannot be seen from inhabited areas. It is truly "hidden behind the ranges." But from where I balanced, atop the summit of the Muztagh Tower—a snow lump no larger than an ordinary eight-by-twelve-inch sheet of paper—K2 rose before me, solitary and majestic, a pyramid with six sharp ridges. It was like seeing a newborn baby for the first time; I experienced a profound longing, a love for that mountain. I knew I had to climb it one day. But I also had to pay attention to where I was standing! With a 10,000-foot drop-off on one side, and an 11,500-foot void on the other, I felt better than ever.

"This is life! This is totally awesome!" I shouted into my tape recorder. I was screaming and howling, and I never wanted these feelings to stop. I was supercharged, lost in a kind of high-altitude, getting-to-the-top ecstasy. And today, when I listen to that tape, the feeling returns. But it also must be said quite clearly and honestly that in climbing there are many other things that I don't like to remember. I'm thirty today, and many of the people I've met along the way never returned from the mountains.

The year following our expedition to Muztagh Tower was tragic. On Broad Peak, a Czech climber ran up to Base Camp and died of altitude sickness. It was a crazy idea he had, running up there like that, ignoring the need to properly acclimatize. But people who die in the mountains often do something unwise, or they are ill prepared. And a few are just plain unlucky. When I see accidents happen in the mountains, and they do happen, it strengthens my resolve to climb carefully.

Yet accidents can strike even the most scrupulously safe climber. My friend Mats Dahlin was never at all careless when we climbed. If my crampons needed to be sharpened when we were up in the mountains, and I didn't have a file, Mats had one. He never forgot anything; he was always well prepared.

We had hoped to scale Cho Oyu in Tibet, but we couldn't get a climbing permit until 1992. In December of 1991, we practiced alpine climbing in Chamonix, France. At Christmastime, there was lots of snow and a hard wind was blowing. From the mountainside, we could see the giant skiing resorts below us. Mats, Svante Yngrot, Petter Johansson, and I climbed simultaneously, swinging our ice axes, kicking in our crampons. The wall was steep. Then a small rock fell from high above. Mats, who was beneath me, was hit by the stone on his temple, just below the rim of his climbing helmet.

At first, I didn't think it was that serious. Then Mats went pale and collapsed. We shook him and shouted at him, but he didn't answer. We decided Svante and Petter should stay with him while I hurried down for help. I descended, then stretched up my arms so that my body formed the letter Y—the international signal for emergency. A helicopter rose into sight and I said a prayer. But the mountain face was too steep and the wind was too strong; the helicopter couldn't reach us.

And Mats left us. He died up there.

The time that followed was horrible. I considered giving up mountaineering, but then I thought, like many climbers before me who have lost a friend in the mountains: "Mats would not have wanted me to stop." Six months later, I went to Nepal and scaled Cho Oyu, my first 8,000-meter peak.

On the flat summit, I took Mats's ice axe from my backpack. A mountaineer's ice axe resembles the Christian cross, and I had attached a picture of Mats and his obituary to it. I stuck the axe in the snow so that it faced the mountain that I could see in the distance.

Mount Everest, Chomolungma.
The Goddess Mother of the World.
The Mountain so high no bird can fly over it.

2

ON EVERY MOUNTAIN TRIP, I have learned something new. Every climb has changed me in some small yet discernible way. For one thing, I grew tired of over-sized climbing expeditions. I could see that the world's tallest mountains were getting infested with people used to luxury—people who used the aid of professional mountain guides, Sherpas, to carry the heavy equipment, and who relied on new technology to reach the top.

But back then, in 1994, I did not yet know Sandy Pittman, the million-dollar mountaineer. Yet I met others who brought their cocktail cabinets and wine cellars to the mountain—and I saw what they left behind: ripped tents, discarded oxygen bottles, old ropes, and empty beer cans. Some campsites looked more like garbage dumps, not places where you'd want to sleep for the night.

Mountaineering, and especially high-altitude climbing, is expensive. And the media have, through their ignorance and "spin," painted mountaineering as an exotic, glamorous, and dangerous sport that now attracts society people. I know, perhaps I shouldn't be so judgmental. Everybody is not like me. But in my opinion, the high-tech gadgets, the abandoned equipment, and the leftover, left-behind junk are a rape of nature. And I am honestly amazed at those climbers who don't see any need for change.

When Edmund Hillary and Tenzing Norgay scaled Mount Everest in 1953, they used every type of equipment available. But the ice axes weighed several pounds back then. The oxygen bottles were as heavy as lead, the climbers wore coarse woolen clothes, and during the approach march, they cooked over wood fires. Nowadays, we have titanium stoves, light as a feather. Ice axes weigh twenty-one ounces, and virtually every other type of gear, clothing, and foodstuff has been revolutionized. Still, it is only human nature that people will make use of any kind of aid or help available in order to reach the top. But to me, this is an outdated concept, like being satisfied with a two-meter high jump in the Olympic Games—as if something that was a great feat in the 1950s should still be so today.

In May 1990, a Swedish team scaled Mount Everest. The expedition made use of almost 400 porters. Their equipment weighed over five tons, and the climbers attained the summit breathing from supplemental oxygen bottles, littering the mountain with the empties. I am not at all interested in that kind of aided, or assisted, climbing.

My heroes are Reinhold Messner and Peter Habeler, the first mountaineers to scale Mount Everest without breathing bottled oxygen. Their landmark ascent was in 1978. Messner believed that if you didn't rely exclusively on your own power during a climb, but made use of gadgets and drugs and too much Sherpa assistance, then you cheated yourself. To Messner, the oxygen mask was like a wall between man and nature. He saw the mountains as something so natural that you didn't have the right—and certainly not any obligation—to conquer them with the aid of technology. Only those who approached the mountains with a humble mind and a purposefully limited selection of technological advancements could experience the harmony of the high peaks.

These were romantic and controversial beliefs—without supplemental oxygen, high-altitude ascents become significantly more dangerous—but I recognized my own reverence for the mountains in his thoughts. Still, Messner's ideas weren't entirely new, either. In the early 1920s, leading British climbers, including several members of the Royal Geographical Society, publicly declared it unethical to climb using supplemental bottled oxygen. Then, in June 1924, Lieutenant Colonel Edward Norton reached an altitude of 28,200 feet on Mount Everest without breathing anything but the mountain's own air.

However, in later years as oxygen bottles got lighter, ideals changed. Soon practically everyone was breathing bottled oxygen while climbing above 26,000 feet (the 8,000-meter level), and that is, more or less, still standard practice on the world's four highest mountains—Everest, K2, Kangchenjunga, and Lhotse. Habeler and Messner broke the trend only briefly, establishing their pure ascent as an example to an elite group. It is also recognized that too much high-altitude climbing without oxygen can potentially damage the brain, so the unpopularity of oxygen-free climbing is entirely understandable.

I must insist, though, that Mount Everest is not 29,028 feet tall if the mountain is scaled by a climber wearing an oxygen mask. The mountain shrinks if bottled oxygen is used, the adventure itself is diminished, and lungs breathing in supplementary oxygen feel an altitude of 26,000 feet to be more like 16,000 feet. Using bottled oxygen is like doping, like taking anabolic steroids. I wanted to climb Everest using only natural means. I wanted to continue along the path that Reinhold Messner had boldly begun to stake out.

Messner was also the first to make a solo ascent of Everest. That was in 1980. Twelve years later, when I drove from Sweden to Tibet in a Range Rover to climb Cho Oyu, I investigated the possibilities of traveling this same route across Europe and Asia by bicycle. Would it be possible to do everything yourself, I wondered, all the way from home to the summit?

Back then I was a military officer, but my goal was to escape the humdrum life at the regiment and climb full-time. To my friends and family, it sounded like a dream. The truth is that many successful climbers have been able to live off the sport, even as far back as the 1950s, and although many star mountaineers died relatively poor, others like the mountaineering giant Messner have become rich giving talks, writing books, and signing sponsorship deals. Nowadays, Messner lives in a castle.

But I was not yet ready for my endeavor to travel alone from Sweden to Mount Everest. In 1993, I joined a Swedish expedition headed for my dream mountain, K2, the world's second-highest peak. No Scandinavian had yet scaled K2, and it occurred to me that if I became the first, I would probably be able to support myself on mountaineering. Therefore, soon after, I backed out of the Swedish K2 expedition and bought "a place" on a Slovenian team going to the peak just prior to the Swedes. Not knowing any of the Slovenian climbers, though, I knew that I was taking a risk. Because in mountaineering, you literally put your life in the hands of your partners; cooperation, working well together, and trust in each other's capabilities are vital.

I was apprehensive before I left for Pakistan, but when I arrived in Islamabad, I was so motivated that I was almost beside myself. I prepared for the ascent by running in the mountains above the city until I felt the taste of blood in my mouth. After a while, a cyst started growing on one of my feet. When it reached the size of a strawberry, I turned to a certain Dr. Haider, who cut it away, placed it in a glass jar, and proudly handed it back to me, just in case I wanted to put it on display on the mantel at home. Since then, unfortunately, I have had no feeling in the upper part of that foot.

In Islamabad I also met Tomaz, the leader of the Slovenian K2 expedition that I had bought into for about $9,000. Tomaz was a youngish guy, rather small, with gray hair. He wore jeans and a T-shirt. When I introduced myself, he looked at me with surprise. My name didn't mean a thing to him. Then his face reddened.

"Kropp?" he stammered. "Oh, yes. That's right. Thanks for your money. You can do whatever you want — but we're climbing without you."

Tomaz had wanted my money only to help fund his expedition. Apart from the cash, he had no interest whatsoever in me. He never even considered letting me climb with his team. His statement was a slap in the face; in fact, it hurt even worse because now I had no one to climb with.

K2 might sound like the name of an income tax return form, but for mountaineers, the name is even more charged than Mount Everest. If Everest is the ultimate ego trophy that millionaire armchair climbers dream about, then K2 is the mountain for real mountaineers. The magical and menacing K2 is probably the most difficult to climb of all the world's fourteen peaks taller than 8,000 meters — 26,247 feet. People who have scaled Everest have come to K2 and died; they had been prepared for the highest mountain in the world, but not for the second highest.

K2, sometimes also called Mount Godwin Austen after an early British explorer, was the second peak in the Karakoram Range whose height was measured. The mountain is situated on the Baltoro Glacier in Pakistan and was first ascended in 1954 by the Italians Lino Lacedelli and Achille Compagnoni — one year after the triumph of Hillary and Norgay on Everest. But K2's climbing history is filled with storms, death, and sorrow. About fifty people have perished on K2 since the peak was first attempted by the Duke of Abruzzi's expedition in 1909.

In the summer of 1986 alone, thirteen people died — almost half of those who were attempting the mountain that season. British mountaineer Jim Curran, one of the fortunate survivors, chronicled the deadly summer in his book *K2: Triumph and*

Tragedy. On August 3 and 4 of that year, eight climbers summitted K2, but very high on the mountain, they were caught in a storm. They took refuge in Camp Four at 26,200 feet. At such an altitude, in what is known as the Death Zone, no one can survive for long, three or four days at the most. Blood circulates much more slowly. You may suffer thrombosis and cerebral edema. And you can cough so hard that you fracture ribs. In August 1986, the storm on K2 raged on and on, but the climbers decided to wait for it to subside — even though days went by and the gale howled with undiminished ferocity.

Everyone in the group had summitted in lightweight style without supplemental oxygen. None of them was inexperienced, certainly not Alan Rouse, who was a legend in the trade. But as the storm continued, the situation became catastrophic. The tents were ripped by the wind, then became buried under the deep snow. And on the morning of August 7, the English climber Julie Tullis died in her sleep. Still, the others remained in camp, even as they ran short of food and gas canisters for cooking. Without propane, they could no longer melt snow for drinking water.

Soon the Austrian Alfred Imitzer was snow-blind and half-mad. His partner, Hannes Wieser, also was delirious, and Rouse, the star mountaineer, talked about how he could melt snow to get water to drink — in his sleeping bag. Not until after being trapped for a week, on August 10, did the climbers make a break for it, but only Kurt Diemberger, Willy Bauer, and the Polish woman mountaineer "Mrufka" Wolf actually left camp. When the storm subsided two days later, only Bauer and Diemberger were alive, and they staggered like walking ghosts into Base Camp.

Seven years later, I hiked to the mountain with my girlfriend, Josephine Beijer. She was not going to climb but would be my support at Base Camp. Josephine was tense and fearful, and I, too, already had ominous thoughts. Not only had my meeting with Tomaz been an ill omen, but I'd experienced a premonition when we caught our first glimpse of K2 from the glacier. The mountain was blown free of snow, showing its cold black rock, and it looked evil and terrifying. It sounds strange, but I see the mountains as living beings, and often they talk to me or warn me. Right then I got the feeling that someone would die on K2 this year, too, and having this knowledge felt like punishment.

Arriving at Base Camp, I tried not to worry about my premonition. Josephine and I pitched our tent and fixed some food. Not far away was Gilkey's Memorial, the somber rock outcropping decorated with commemorative plaques to those who had died on the mountain. This year, K2 Base Camp was a nylon tent town housing ten expeditions. That night, I walked around and said hello to everyone.

I was happily relieved to meet David Sharman, an English climber who, like me, had also bought into the Slovenian team — and been fooled. David and I hit it off, and we decided to climb together. When I told him I was hoping to become the first Scandinavian to surmount K2, he countered, "Al Rouse was the first Englishman to summit, but I'm going to be the first one to get back down, too." He didn't say this in a cynical way but spoke soberly, like a man with a fixed purpose. We both knew the stakes.

One day, the Slovenian expedition set off for the top. At noon, we heard them on the radio: "One hour left to summit," they said.

Of course we were happy for them. But then the almost predictable storm broke, and there was no more word from them. Later that night we heard news that all six climbers were huddling in a two-person tent flapping wildly in the gale. Then Bostian, a major in the Slovenian army, suffered cerebral edema. The others tried to carry and pull him downhill, but he died on the Shoulder — the same haunted place where everyone perished in 1986. Now Bostian lay in the snow, with a long rope tied around his body. I climbed up to help the survivors. I climbed hard, and after ascending House's Chimney, a 100-foot-high vertical cleft, I reached a narrow ledge and Camp Two. Three of the Slovenians were there, listless, haggard, and barely able to stand.

"It doesn't matter any longer," they told me. "We failed." Stiepe was snow-blind. One of Boris's toes was frostbitten, as were all of Zvonko's toes and fingers. I helped them into the tent. There was only room for half the tent on the ledge, so we crawled inside, pressed our backs up against the rock face, and dangled our feet over the edge.

Life might just as well have already ended for them, the Slovenians were so dejected and defeated. When I asked them to do this or help with that, they answered: "It's no use. We're too tired." Zvonko, the poor devil, held out his hands for me to inspect. They were black and covered with frostbite blisters. I removed his boots and saw that his feet, too, from the ankles down, were frozen solid. Then I placed his feet under my armpits to warm them, and we sat like that all night long while I spoke to them in a soothing tone as the tent flapped in the wind. Perhaps I saved an inch or two of Zvonko's feet; I don't know. They were all apathetic that night—as often happens to people who become frostbitten—but they still glanced uneasily at each other when I asked them: "Did you reach the top?"

"No," they replied, after hesitating for a moment. Zvonko had gotten the closest. He turned back 200 feet from the summit of K2.

Back home, Boris eventually had two toes amputated, and Zvonko lost all ten of his fingers and all ten toes. But then, in order to recoup the expedition's finances and I suppose their honor, the Slovenians made a desperate decision. They fabricated a story that they had reached the summit. It was a miserable lie, of course, one that poisons mountaineering.

David Sharman and I prepared for our own summit bid. We headed up the Abruzzi Spur a week later and reached Camp Four on the ill-fated plateau at 26,200 feet on August 22. The weather, surprisingly, was nice. It had stopped snowing, and for once there wasn't much wind. David complained about a headache. We crept into our sleeping bags early and tried to breathe calmly.

When climbing tall mountains, you must rise extremely early at the last camp, so you will have time to get to the summit and back down before dark. I left at 3:00 A.M.; David started shortly after me. When the sun appeared in the sky, David sat far beneath me with his head down. It turned out that he had slipped and fractured something. He gave up. I was alone now as I approached the Bottleneck, a steep famous passage that is the crux on K2's normal route. Many climbers, overcome by grogginess in this difficult section, have slipped and fallen to their deaths. But now, as I climbed solo through the Bottleneck, everything went smoothly—as if this wasn't at all the notorious K2 but some other, ordinary mountain.

At 11:10 A.M., I stood alone on the summit of K2, the mountain of mountains. "I made it!" I shouted out in a cracked, dry voice. I got my camera from my backpack and took pictures of the view and of myself, my face burned red by the sun, the hoarfrost covering my nose and beard.

"What a star I am!" I thought. "I've climbed the hardest peak in the world without any problems."

But at that very same moment, I felt the power of the mountain. This icy cold awareness of the mountain's immensity came as a response to my thoughts, which I instantly regretted. The mountain—I felt it clearly now—would punish me for my pride. When I turned around, I saw ominous black clouds drifting toward me.

"Time is short. I have to get down to Camp Three before the storm hits. Then I might survive," I thought. I immediately started climbing back down the summit snow ridge. Then one of my crampons came off. I fell and went flying down an icy slope, desperately groping for my ice axe. After falling 100 feet, I grabbed my axe, self-arrested, and managed to stop.

"Hell!" I shouted out loud. "What am I doing?"

I stood on a precarious ice field sloped at a 45-degree angle, I was still above the notorious Bottleneck, and a blizzard was approaching. I plunged the axe into the ice, and then I sat on it. My heart was pounding, and with numbed hands I fumbled to put my crampon back on. My hands were suddenly so cold that it was a hopeless task, maybe impossible. But finally, I snapped it back on. I did not want to become a part of K2, so with the fear of death, I slowly down-climbed through the Bottleneck back to the Shoulder, to safety, sort of.

I reached Camp Four just as the storm slapped me. The strong winds nearly blew me off my feet, and I realized to my chagrin that everything was exactly as it had been at the start of the 1986 tragedy. But they had been eight — and I was alone. David was nowhere to be seen; he must have already descended. I crawled into my tent. I saw some fresh blood, my blood. I was bleeding from somewhere. I had to think the situation through very carefully. "Try to remember Curran's goddamn book," I said to myself.

I slid into my sleeping bag and lay on my back. The storm pressed the tent nylon right up against my nose. I was breathing rapidly and irregularly. My heart was pounding; I was close to panic. "Calm down and be rational," I told myself, "and remember 1986. Don't repeat the mistake they made, waiting for the storm to pass! Just gather yourself together and get down!" I wasn't hungry at all, but I forced myself to eat every scrap of food I could find, then I took out my Walkman and listened to some samba, the happiest music I had. The tent was warped and about to burst at the seams, but in the middle of all this, I felt the groove. "Samba! Yeah, samba!" I yelled into the wind, trying to create an illusion of harmony.

The following morning, the storm raged just as hard. The edge of the plateaulike Shoulder ended in a 10,000-foot precipice. Earlier, we'd marked out the way to a ridge some 600 feet away from the tent, placing marker sticks every 80 feet. From that ridge, you could make your way back down the Abruzzi Spur to Base Camp. I got out of the tent and stood up in the waist-high snow. I couldn't see anything—no bamboo wands, no nothing. Everything was a white, whipping fog.

"It's no use," I muttered and returned to the tent. Then I remembered that Bostian, the one who died from cerebral edema, had died here. "He has the rope tied around him that they used to drag him down with," I thought. "But where is he?"

I began to dig desperately, rummaging through the snow near the tent, panting heavily. Finally I found something—a large object. It was Bostian's backpack. "But the rope? Where is the rope?" Anxiously, I opened up the rucksack and, aha! A rope. I was glad I didn't have to find Bostian himself.

I tied one end of the rope to my tent, and myself to the rope, then used the rope as a tether so I could search for the marker wands and still find my way back to the tent. But I could hardly move through the great mass of snow. It took me four hours to find the first stick. But even once I'd found it, I realized I was stuck. I was about to be buried alive in the snow. I couldn't go anywhere, and I couldn't see anything. "Now it's over!" I thought. "I will die." But I think then the mountain sensed my feeling of complete despair, and, miraculously, a gap in the snowy fog opened up just long enough so that I saw the bamboo marker wands leading across the next snow slope to the descent ridge.

I threw myself down on my belly onto the snow and slid forward. I kept moving forward and descending. I staggered downhill as day and night merged. I ran out of food and water. I ate snow, which I knew was crazy—it causes diarrhea—and I came upon tents that had been torn down by the wind, their poles snapped in half. I knew that an avalanche might come at any moment. I sensed that the mountain still wanted to take something from me, perhaps not my life, but something else that meant a great deal to me.

At Camp One, I heard the characteristic warning: a loud clap. A roar and a rumble followed, and an enormous amount of snow shot toward me with terrific force. The avalanche passed me at a distance of 300 feet, but the wind blast threw me some fifteen or twenty feet until the fixed rope I was tied to stopped my fall. But at that moment, the videotape with all my film sequences fell out of my backpack. It fell into the avalanche, which flowed out over the glacier below, up the side of the adjacent mountain, Broad Peak, then washed back toward K2. That was it. The mountain had taken the tape from me, the videotape that was supposed to be my livelihood when I returned home. K2 had shown its power.

Not much later, I broke through the snow crust and fell into a small glacial lake. Standing in water up to my waist, I was instantly chilled to the marrow. Once I'd gotten out of the water, I lay down beneath a sheltering boulder, shivering with hypothermia. Large snowflakes were falling, the visibility was very poor, and there was more than just a small chance of other deadly avalanches falling. Thinking about hot food, I forced myself to tear off my sodden outer clothes and wring them out, and then I fell asleep in my sleeping bag.

When I awoke, twenty-eight hours had passed since I'd left Camp Four. I didn't know where I was. But suddenly — to my complete surprise — I saw a multicolored town appear through the fog. I almost had to laugh. Unknowingly, I'd slept some 600 feet from Base Camp.

I took my radio and called: "Göran Kropp here!"

I heard surprise in the voice that answered: "We thought you were dead."

My girlfriend, Josephine Beijer, had also thought I had died, and when I walked into camp like someone risen from the dead, she met me, harrowed and weeping.

"Göran! Göran!" she cried. "Are you really alive?"

Later, I realized that I had lost her on K2. Josephine just couldn't live with that kind of worry, and when she understood that I was planning to continue my high-altitude climbing, she left me, or maybe I should say we broke up.

But that was in the future. Now, in Base Camp, I ate a sandwich of Swedish caviar, drank a Slovenian beer, and fell into a deep, sixteen-hour-long sleep.

3

THE DAY I GOT TO THE Swedish embassy in Islamabad, I understood that I could make a livelihood out of mountaineering. My climb of K2 had created a huge interest. At home, I quit my military job, formed my company, Kropp & Äventyr, and began lecturing to earn a living. Over Christmas of 1993, Magnus Nilsson and I went to Kaga Tondo in Mali where we scaled a few vertical rock peaks that rise hundreds of feet above the Sahara. The next year, I saw K2 once again, but it was not for the reason I would have wished.

Daniel Bidner was considered to be one of Sweden's best all-round climbers. He was a member of the 1993 Swedish K2 expedition that I had initially belonged to. During his descent from the summit, something happened to Daniel below the Bottleneck. He told his climbing partner, Anders Rafael Jensen: "I see Swedish flags and red cabins." Then Daniel sat down to rest for a moment, lost his balance, and tumbled and fell down the precipice. It all happened in an instant.

In 1994 I was in Pakistan once again, this time to scale Broad Peak (26,400 feet) with a team including Mats Holmgren and

Nicolas Gafgo. We hoped to climb the mountain from the south, which no one had done before. But I also had a promise to keep to Daniel Bidner's family. One day I hiked the four miles of difficult terrain farther up the moraines to K2 Base Camp. In my rucksack I carried a plaque with Daniel's name on it.

It was strange to be back. Everything looked virtually the same, as if nothing had happened, and no time had passed. I walked slowly up to the Gilkey memorial rock and placed Daniel's plaque among the many others, each imprinted with the names of climbers who died on K2. It was an extremely sad moment. There were so many names, so many memorials. But I felt Daniel's spirit was with me, and I wondered, not for the last time, why we had chosen to lead such a dangerous life.

All of my adult life the mountains have called out to me with their majesty and inspiration, to come and worship at their throne of natural beauty. Through my reverence for the mountains I have gained the strength necessary to overcome my fear of them and to accept the risks involved in climbing them. When I am in the mountains, I often feel intoxicated with freedom. It is a complete freedom of experience and a freedom of choice. Neither Mats Dahlin nor Daniel was careless or foolhardy. They were living the life they chose, but I also saw that my friends had died tragically, so I prepared myself as meticulously as possible to avoid any unnecessary risk.

As my self-confidence increased, my driving force became the desire to do things that others called impossible. I had a well-grounded faith in my dreams, but if I saw that a venture was hopeless, I abandoned it without regret. Our expedition never scaled Broad Peak from the south. At 21,000 feet, we turned around — but a week later I made the summit alone, via the normal route, after a final push of nearly eighteen hours. And in the back of my mind, calling my name and summoning me, was Mount Everest.

The main idea in my dreams about climbing Everest was to do everything in the most natural way possible—and to use only my own power. I considered how to get to the mountain. Gasoline-powered engines were out of the question. But riding a horse . . . ? Or how about walking . . . ?

I decided to bike to Everest.

I also planned to make my climb without using bottled oxygen or porters to carry my supplies, and during the climb, I would eat only the food and use only the equipment that I had brought with me on the bicycle from Sweden. When I applied for a permit to climb Mount Everest—the permit cost $50,000 for seven people—there was a five-year waiting list for the standard South Col route. So next I contacted Rob Hall, a distinguished climber and guide from New Zealand, who was on his way to Everest with a group of well-to-do Americans, and I asked if I could buy into his permit. Rob kindly declined, so I chose another, slightly more difficult route—Everest's South Pillar.

At the same time, I began calculating the costs. The figure I ended up with was $350,000, so the next step was to raise money. I picked up the telephone book, the business directory. Then I sat down and opened to the first page. Would AAAAA Office Chairs be interested in sponsoring me? Or A.A.—Alcoholics Anonymous? I guessed probably not. But the multinational company ABB ought to have a few pennies to spare. I kept going like that. I called 320 companies that seemed to have some kind of connection to my project, and I sent them brochures and material, but people told me no, no, no.

Or they said: "Sounds great! Really interesting. But forgive me for being frank with you: We don't think you'll make it."

Some people wanted to meet me. I met with representatives from the chocolate company Cloetta three times, but the only thing they offered was chocolate at wholesale price—as if I was going to open a candy store! Other companies explained that they didn't sponsor individuals.

At the same time, I tried to make some time for biking—I wasn't all that much of a cyclist. But it was hopeless; the chase for sponsors and money took all my time.

"In due time, I'll get to go cycling," I thought.

One day while giving a lecture, I noticed a beautiful, sharp-looking young woman with a strange last name that began with the letter C. I didn't think much more about her, not until she took my climbing course. But then she joined my hang-gliding course in Slovakia, the summer before I went to Mount Everest. This time she helped me out, since she spoke Czech fluently. Renata Chlumska was her name. She had been a model in Paris and was just generally irresistible. Her parents were from Czechoslovakia, and I hired her to work for me. I was in love.

We worked together to prepare my Everest-by-bicycle expedition. In total, we signed with fourteen sponsors, the largest of which was the telecommunication company Ericsson. Another firm, Informedia, would issue press releases detailing my progress while I was gone. And we struck deals with the morning paper *Svenska Dagbladet,* with TV3, and with Radio P4. I was supposed to give live reports on the radio every week. But still we needed more money, so we had no choice but to start cutting the budget, from $350,000 down to $240,000. In the end, I still had to take out a $40,000 bank loan.

Then came the packing hysteria. I couldn't afford to bring one single ounce that wasn't necessary if I had to transport it by bike from Sweden to Kathmandu, and then carry it to Everest Base Camp—not a single unnecessary piece of food, not an extra pair of underwear. After all, I could turn the ones I was wearing inside out quite a few times! I sat with my packing lists day and night, asking myself over and over: Do I really need more than one pair of socks? Aren't two pairs of mittens enough?

Since I wanted to carry everything myself—my food, camping equipment, and technical climbing gear—on the approach march from just outside of Kathmandu up to Mount Everest, that section would also be very tough. I had to minimize everything. I definitely wanted to avoid hiring porters, and after endless brooding, I brought one climbing helmet, two ice axes, one rope, one harness, three ice screws, two locking carabiners, five chocks, and one grigri belay device. I also packed three sewn slings, one sixteen-foot accessory cord, one pair of climbing boots, two adjustable-length ski poles, one portable stove and cookset, one food thermos, one Victorinox knife, a one-gallon waterbag, and several propane canisters for the stove.

My biggest problem was food. In Europe and Asia, I planned to buy my food along the way, but while on the mountain, I would only eat the freeze-dried food I brought from Sweden. I contemplated how much food I would need and whether freeze-dried food alone provided enough nourishment for someone who was going to scale Mount Everest—without supplemental oxygen to boot. I hoped so! I took 32 freeze-dried main courses, 112 freeze-dried soups, 56 drinks with dextrose, 56 chocolate drinks, 48 packages of crackers, 28 chocolate bars, 5 packages of dextrose, a dozen Power Bars, and finally a package of breakfast gruel.

The next item I needed was a bicycle. I chose an Ultima, which was provided to me by the bicycle manufacturer Crescent. I spent two days learning how to repair it in all conceivable ways. I packed a cycle pump, a multipurpose tool, a monkey wrench, a pair of pliers, a spoke adjuster, a tool for taking the chain apart, a tire remover, and a hexagonal wrench.

Then I packed everything onto my bike trailer, along with an Avocet bicycle meter, two bicycle locks, three inner tubes, fifty spokes, four brake shoes, and one spare rear wheel. I had one tent, two backpacks, one kit bag, one sleeping bag, one ground pad, one outer layer of clothing, one fleece sweater, and five pairs of socks. I packed one pair of gloves, one pair of shell mittens, one hat, Javlin pile salopettes, one set of Termo underwear, two sets of Termo light underwear, one set of Craft underwear, and a few other things.

Then there was the cell phone, a Fuji camera, a Nikon FE2 camera, one lens, extra film, a camcorder, video tape, a Glocom satellite telephone, a Walkman, five cassette tapes, rechargeable batteries and a charger, and medication for pain and frostbite. That was it. Whatever else there was, I left it at home.

In October of 1995, the Swedish newspapers were writing about Vice Prime Minister Mona Sahlin's alleged abuse of her government-issued credit card. On October 16, after a period a silence, Sahlin gave a fervent speech in her defense, and the tabloids printed extra editions.

"I have not been wangling!" she declared from the front pages.

The same day, I rolled my bicycle up the hill to the end of Yttersta Tvärgränd on the southern island of Stockholm, past eighteenth-century houses and two day-care centers. This was my starting point, and the media was waiting for me. I glanced out over the water. It was a beautiful fall day. Soon it was 1:00 P.M., and below the hill was the busy Ringvägen street.

I'd been up since 5:00 A.M., talking on a television morning show, and when I arrived at my starting point, cameras were snapping. My good friend Per Calleberg gave a welcoming speech, and I posed in front of my bike, answering questions. I was upbeat.

"Yes, it's very cold on Mount Everest."

"Yes, there are sometimes hurricanes, that's true."

"No, I don't regret the trip now!"

I especially remember a young blond reporter from *Expressen*, a Swedish tabloid. She had a very aggressive tone of voice, as if she wanted to call my bluff.

"What's the point of doing everything on your own," she asked, "when you will be using the same routes and ladders that others have put in place in the Icefall?"

The Khumbu Icefall is the most dangerous section of the Khumbu Glacier as it flows downhill sandwiched between Mount Everest's West Shoulder and Nuptse, a neighboring peak. All climbers must pass through this lethal zone to reach Camp One at 19,600 feet. The Icefall is renowned as the most dangerous place on Everest. It moves slowly, breaking apart like a sluggish sea of icebergs, and now and then its great ice towers collapse. Many climbers have died in the Khumbu Icefall — falling into crevasses or being crushed to death by falling ice — and all climbers have great respect for this haunted place. At the start of each climbing season, the route through the Icefall is established by a team of Sherpas who fix ropes and ladders up it before the various expeditions arrive.

I was mildly annoyed by her question. "What is that tabloid woman saying?" I thought to myself. "Will I be selling out my principles if I follow the same route as everybody else?"

"Then I guess I'll have to go a different way!" I said.

I didn't think any more about it right then. I wolfed down a sandwich and some pea soup, said a final good-bye to Renata and other friends, then rolled down toward Ringvägen street, turned into Hornsgatan, crossed the bridge, and headed for the town of Södertälje.

"Finally," I thought. "I'm on my way."

People honked their horns and waved at me as I rode along. A middle-aged man leaned out of his car window. "If I were your age, I would do exactly the same thing. It must be great just setting out like that."

The first day, I biked thirty-eight miles, and at the church in Hölö, I pitched my tent. It was a great moment. My head was still buzzing, but I felt myself growing peaceful, and I realized how long

I had been waiting for this, waiting to just have time to myself. Later, people would ask me what I thought about during all those hours on the bike, and some wondered if the loneliness didn't drive me crazy. But I had my entire life to think through, and I enjoyed having the time to do it.

Next morning, when I set off at 7:40, I felt as if I was on a triumphant march. People cheered me on and took pictures, and at a café in the small town of Vagnhärad, I was invited in for lunch. But there were lots of hills, too, the fall wind was blowing, and my knees and thighs hurt.

"This is ridiculous, Göran," I thought. "I just started, but I hurt so bad I could die."

I decided to look back rather than forward and not let myself be discouraged by the endless miles ahead. But while the landscape swished by, I couldn't help getting a little bit worried. I knew my game plan well: "I have to be in Kathmandu by March — and I have 7,800 miles to go! Can I make it? Or will the whole project fail?"

That night, my second, I slept by a sewage treatment plant outside the town of Norrköping. The rain pattered against the tent nylon, and when the wind brought the stench from the sewage in, I wrote in my journal, like an incantation: "We'll start out with new energy tomorrow. Forward!"

The next day, a storm hit, and I left the open landscape and opted for smaller roads protected by their surrounding woods — but these roads turned out to be hopeless; my wheels skidded on the slippery surface. Sometimes, I would take a break and tell the local press that everything was great. But actually my legs were really hurting, especially my left calf. "I'm not fit enough," I thought. "I've gotten out of shape."

It didn't occur to me that the pain was because I was pedaling in a pair of boots. I had still not received my cycling shoes (Salomon, size 11). Somewhere outside the village of Tofta, I was met by Renata, who gave me the shoes, and luckily the pain started to subside. On October 23, after a night at an inn, I rolled onboard the ferry between Trelleborg in Sweden and Rostock in Germany. In the sauna on the ferry, I met a Polish jazz trombonist who had played in a jazz club in Finland and was now headed for Prague. He was big and fat, wore glasses, and had a mustache, and to me he really looked like a jazz trombonist. He couldn't have been anything else. And he probably thought: "Hmm, so this is the guy cycling to Everest."

In a village in Germany, on Road 108 leading toward Neubrandeburg, one of my tires got totally shredded along the rim by the cobblestone streets. But that was a minor problem. In Zossen in eastern Germany, I wrote in my journal:

> *I'm getting into a routine. I bike eighteen or twenty miles. Then I rest, stretch, and eat. Then another twenty miles, and then it's time for lunch, and at the same time I buy breakfast for the next day. I finish off the day by cycling at least another twenty miles, and shortly after 5:00 P.M., I pitch camp.*

Zossen was a deserted Russian military town, a sad place that time had left behind, full of locked-up barracks and empty buildings. I sensed a certain anarchy that came naturally to the people who still lived here. Whatever the military had left behind, they claimed as their own and took it home.

I didn't need road signs or the odometer to tell me that I'd gotten far away from home; the poverty told me. It started in eastern Germany, then increased slowly through the Czech Republic and Slovakia. It took a break in progressive Hungary, then returned in full force in the misery and concrete ghettos of Rumania.

Between Dorog and Dabas in Hungary, the first wet snow fell. It was a real storm. I was soaking wet and very cold, but there was nothing around me but forests and fields, nothing, that is, until finally I saw a little sign with a bed and the text: "Three miles."

The road was covered with wet sleet. I arrived at a ramshackle house in the middle of nowhere. It was after dark, and a faint light glowed in one window. I had a strange premonition, but I jumped off my bike anyway, walked up to the door, and stepped right into a drama. I had interrupted a very heated conversation; that was my first impression. Second, everybody was staring at me as if I came from outer space. But perhaps I did look like an alien from Saturn, clad in my red windbreaker and flashy cycling clothes.

Three women were in the room. All of them wore leather skirts, studded belts, fishnet stockings, and stiletto high heels. Beside them sat a group of nervous-looking men who appeared to be guarding the women. I had come to a brothel.

At the far end of the room were a bar and a number of doors which I guessed led to love nests. But I got the feeling that the men weren't on just an ordinary visit to these prostitutes, but rather that they were involved in some complicated intrigue that had been going on for some time.

"Do you have any vacancies?" I asked quietly. I was too tired to bike any farther.

"No!" said several voices in unison.

"What about a cup of tea then? I need to get warm."

The women glanced at each other. One nodded. I walked up to the bar; all eyes were riveted on me. Perhaps because I looked so strange, or just very innocent, their initial hostility was soon replaced by curiosity. Everyone sat down around me; they now seemed genuinely interested in who I was.

"Where are you going?" one woman asked.

She might have been thirty. Her heavy eye makeup had run a little, as if she'd been crying. I braced myself for their response to my preposterous story.

"I'm going to cycle to Nepal and climb Mount Everest," I answered cautiously. They stared at me in silence, trying to figure out if I was joking. When they realized I was serious, pandemonium broke out. Everyone began talking at once, shouting and gesturing, and in the midst of the confusion, someone demanded to see my bike, and the prostitutes ran out into the snow in their stiletto high heels to get it. Everybody was screaming and laughing and sliding around in the slush, and the bike was carried inside like a triumphant chariot — or a war trophy. I unfolded my map of the world and showed them my route.

"This is where I'm going," I said and put my finger on Kathmandu, while everyone squeezed together around me, with their fishnet stockings, mustaches, and ample bosoms.

"But, my God, it's winter! Are you really going to bike all that way?" the madam asked in a motherly tone. Then, without waiting for my response, she graciously declared that I could stay for the night.

The men, I learned, came from Turkey and were on their way home, but their Fiat had broken down a week earlier. They had ended up here, had been swept up in a complicated love drama, and had stopped caring about fixing the car. Now the brothel was full of jealous eyes, and only the madam herself seemed to be above the intrigue.

She continued looking at me, as if contemplating something.

"I have a surprise for you," she said and disappeared.

She returned with a young woman with dyed black hair, also clad in regulation stiletto heels, leather miniskirt, a fishnet top, studded belt, and fishnet stockings. She sure had all the paraphernalia, but she looked as embarrassed as a school girl. She stole furtive glances at me, then looked down, scraping her high heels nervously on the floor.

"This is my daughter," the madam said, making gestures in the air with indecent innuendo as well as motherly pride. "And of course, it's all on the house," she added, giving me a generous smile.

I couldn't believe what she'd said, and I hurried to say, as politely as I could: "Thank you, thank you, but no, I have to get some sleep."

I hurried into the room where the Turks were staying. I slept fitfully until a clamoring of voices woke me up around midnight. I jumped out of bed. Out in the main room, I heard screams and fighting. A male voice shouted something about passports and the police. I went to check on my bike and equipment but was met instead by a harrowed crowd.

Chairs had been knocked over and a bottle smashed. One of the Turks stood by the bar, unshaved, in a gray shirt with large sweat stains under his armpits. He was smoking a cigarette. The women were gathered in a corner. Two were crying. In the middle of the room, a squat policeman stood scribbling down notes. The Turks, it turned out, had been fighting with knives. The aggression was still palpable, but no one had been seriously hurt—with the exception of one man who seemed to be severely confused.

"Lenin, Stalin, okay?" he said to me, as if the most natural thing for us to talk about right then was old dictators. For the sake of peace, I went along with whatever he said. We were in total agreement, although it was unclear exactly what we had agreed upon.

That morning, everyone was still in the bar. No one appeared to have slept a wink. The madam looked at me, gave a tired smile, and waved me off with a sweep of her hand. I didn't have to pay, she said. I got on my bike and left, thinking that the Turks would probably stay there for all eternity.

Out on a muddy side road that led to the E75, I had a flat tire. When I sat down to repair it, a passing car splashed mud and sludge all over me.

It was November 7, 1995, and I had covered 1,300 miles.

I was in Rumania when winter approached. The roads were dismal, and sometimes my feet grew numb on the ice-cold bike pedals. One night, the juice in my water bottle froze. The poverty here made me feel unsafe. The gazes people gave me were no longer curious but hungry. It was strange to encounter this other Europe, a Europe so gray and impoverished.

In the town of Turnu, people dumped their wrecked cars and trash right into the Danube River. I saw vast fields where nothing grew but weeds, and ghostlike slums where people lived in run-down concrete tenements. On November 12, I took a cold and drafty hotel room for the night. I complained about it being too cold, but the only thing the owner could give me was a contraption made of glowing electrical coils and a stone. In the middle of the night I smelled smoke and woke up to find a fire in my "heater." I switched off the electricity, and the next morning when I left, I was totally fed up. But life continued to reveal itself to me in unexpected ways. That same day, it seemed like the entire country of Rumania had gotten married! I met countless wedding processions on my route and watched people give salutes, firing guns or waving their hats, for the newlyweds.

On November 18, a woman in a Trabant hit my bike trailer. Two days later, the trailer broke down. I managed to get it repaired for very little money at a Shell station in Luleburgaz.

On November 25, I got a flat back tire.

On the 27th, in a hotel in Bolu, I got sick to my stomach. The same day, though, I could at last smell that mountains were again getting near. Snow-covered peaks rose in the area to an altitude of over 11,000 feet. I had to fight back my impatience and feelings of longing. I still had a very, very long way to go before I could start climbing.

On the 29th, two spokes in my rear wheel broke, and my cell phone wouldn't work. On the afternoon of the 30th, up ahead, I saw a white Suzuki with its indicator lights flashing. Next to the car stood a man, and at his side, a very beautiful woman. It was my filmmaker, Fredrik Blomqvist, and lovely Renata—Team Sweden—who magically appeared now and then to film me.

With Renata in my tent, I didn't get started until late in the mornings. I also didn't care. Life didn't have to be all suffering. These were nice times. But I began to worry. Will people get the idea that Fredrik and Renata are helping me, that I just tag along after the car with the film team? Never! And sadly, I got a bit edgy toward Renata. When she innocently bought me a couple of bananas, I blurted out, "Are you out of your mind? This is a solo expedition. I can't accept help from anyone!" Another day, when one of my saddle bags fell off the bike and rolled down a slope, Renata, who was driving behind me, stopped and stepped out of her car to retrieve it.

"Don't touch it!" I shouted, as if she were about to cause a disaster. "I'll pick it up."

Still, I was not always completely orthodox, going by my self-imposed rules. I wanted to be entirely self-propelled to Everest, but I decided that I wouldn't swim across rivers or seas. So, I had already cheated twice, I felt, by taking ferries, and on my birthday, December 11, in Horasan, I ate a chocolate bar that I didn't purchase myself. It was given to me as a gift.

On December 13, I was cycling across eastern Turkey, heading for the Iranian border. I wasn't far from Kurdistan. I began to hear shots being fired. Perhaps it was a restless soldier from the Turkish army practicing his marksmanship. There were bullet holes in every road sign I passed; you'd think they were intended as targets rather than signposts showing the way.

Wild dogs ran after me, too, snapping at my trailer. But then I began to encounter the most dangerous phenomenon that would recur throughout the rest of my trip: boys throwing stones at me. Why is stone throwing by young boys such an international pastime? After a while, I decided to return the fire, with hard and well-aimed throws. I wanted to give them a little experience-based learning.

The Turkish countryside was beautiful. The landscape was

hilly and rather barren, but still, I often passed fields decorated by a thin frost. Northeast of Lake Van, I saw the Ararat Massif, mentioned in Genesis:

> And the ark rested in the seventh month, on the seventeenth day of the month, upon the mountains of Ararat. And the waters decreased continually until the tenth month: in the tenth month, on the first day of the month were the tops of the mountains seen.

So, in a way, life after the Great Flood began with mountain climbing.

But Ararat doesn't lure only Bible-thumping archaeologists. I dreamed of climbing the mountain while I cycled along a snowy road below it on my way to the town of Dogubayazit, close to the Iranian border. Night fell. Far away, I glimpsed the lights of the town. Everything was still—until the soldier in me heard an all-too-familiar metallic sound which made me jump. I knew what was happening even before I had time enough to formulate the words: An automatic weapon was being loaded. I instantly threw up my hands above the handlebars and shouted: "No problem!" knowing full well that the person holding the gun might not be in agreement.

I could not see the person who answered in Turkish. The next moment, a blind shot went off.

"Damn!" I thought. "Now what's happening?" I edged closer to the roadside ditch, ready to throw myself into it. Thoughts were buzzing in my head: "Is it a Kurdish liberation army supporter who wants publicity? A nervous Turkish soldier? Who is shooting at me?"

The night was very dark. After a little while, I heard people walking toward me. Three Turkish soldiers appeared. They acted as if nothing had happened. I could hardly make them out in the darkness. One of them lit a cigarette, and while his face was illuminated by the flame, he tried to look like an American movie actor he'd seen on television. All three of them were playing some macho theater. But mostly, it seemed like they were bored and just trying to pass the time.

"Yes, yes. I'm on my way," I finally told them, extremely annoyed, and biked off toward Dogubayazit. I got a room for the night there. A sticker on the wall read: "Ararat Mountain Expedition." My odometer said 3,163 miles.

4

IN IRAN, DOGS CHASED ME
and boys threw stones at me, too. But there was a new kind of car
here that I'd never seen. Called a Pelikan, it was a British car that
had totally failed on the European market in the 1960s. The Iranian government apparently bought them all for a song. The
Pelikan looked a lot like a Ford Cortina—if you wanted to say
something nice about it—and it wasn't very fast, which on my bike
I appreciated. A Pelikan is what the Trabant is in eastern Germany,
the Skoda is in the Czech Republic and Slovakia, the Lada is in
Rumania and Bulgaria, and the old Renaults are in Turkey. The
Pelikan is the Iranian Volkswagen: the people's car. Like all good
European vehicles, it has migrated southward, drawn to the
warmer weather.

Just look at the Mercedes! You buy it new in Frankfurt or
London, then it reappears in Belgrade or Sofia, later perhaps in
Amman, and finally, when the doors are about to fall off, it's
driven by a well-to-do gangster in Somalia. In India, there are
quite a few old Rolls-Royces from the 1920s, with oak wheels and
lamps that you light with a cigarette lighter. These cars carry an

air about them of the olden days; they transport us back into another era.

But Iran was not just an earlier time—it was another world entirely. At least it was for me, a male and a Westerner who was permitted to see only the exterior facade. Why did Khomeini look so evil on all those giant billboards? Who'd come up with the cute idea of painting flowers growing out of hand grenades? And what artist thought that two Kalashnikovs, laid out like crossbones, make such a good match with a dove of peace that you have to paint this image all over the place?

On the other hand, many Iranians were very nice. They wanted to invite me to their homes—but first they had to get a permit. Permission from whom, I wondered. But once they'd gotten the necessary papers signed, they asked me about everything: How do I live? How much do I earn?

"And how many kids?"

"Zero!"

"No kids? Something wrong with the machinery?" the men asked. Giggle, giggle.

Other Iranians appeared to be in a state of mass psychosis. They threw stones at me, and they threw them hard, as if they wanted to kill me. And maybe they did, but now I threw stones back, which made me feel really good. When a boy tried to put a stick into my bicycle wheel, I tried to kick him.

December 18

ROUTE: QARAHCHMAN—MIANEH—TEHRAN

I spend the night in a hostel. I wake to the truck driver next to me saying his morning prayers. It's been snowing, and outside, dogs are barking. I put on warm clothes, and for a moment I consider putting on my climbing helmet as protection against stone throwing, then I decide not to.

When I start cycling, my rear wheel seems a little warped. They have put salt on the roads during the night. The temperature warms, the snow melts, and after a while, I stop and buy Iranian nougat. I discover that three spokes have detached from the rim — the same problem I encountered in Turkey — but now I don't have a spare rim. I'm in trouble.

Six miles later, the rim collapses, and I'm stranded on the outskirts of the desert. Damn! I catch a ride with a truck driver to Mianeh, but people in the village shake their heads when I show them the bike.

"Only in Tehran can they fix it!" they say.

I take a bus to Tehran and get a room in a luxury hotel, with the standard Iranian slogan "Down with the USA" written in large letters on the wall. That night, I'm haunted by nervous thoughts. I imagine how people in Sweden will shrug their shoulders: "That guy Kropp, did you hear he cheated? Yes, he took a bus for 300 miles, from Mianeh to Tehran."

December 19

ROUTE: TEHRAN—MIANEH

I wake up early. I've decided to go back to Mianeh as soon as the wheel is fixed. I'm not going to cheat. That morning, I find a wonderful repairman who fixes the wheel for free.

"You are my guest," he says. He seems very proud to have me as his customer. He looks around in his shop for a long time for something to give me, and finally he finds a mask and a travel guide to Turkey in French. He hands them over solemnly.

I take the bus to Mianeh, and late that night, I crawl into my sleeping bag close to the place where the rim collapsed. I'm ashamed of myself. How could I even think about not going back and biking those 300 miles?

Christmas Eve
ROUTE: KARAJ—TEHRAN

I have Christmas lunch with the Swedish ambassador, Hans Andersson, and his wife, Eva. I almost start crying when I see the Christmas buffet: meatballs, beet salad, even herring. It's like a dream. Dag from the embassy is Santa Claus. Hans, the ambassador, plays piano, and I accompany him on recorder. Afterward, Dag and I visit the British embassy, which resembles a fortress. Once the Americans left Tehran, the British became the most vilified people there. On several occasions, bombs have been thrown over the walls. In the embassy courtyard, I see an Iranian woman. I flinch. The tip of her nose has been cut off. Her eyes are sad. Her head is bent.

"Did you see her?" I softly ask Dag.

"She worked at the British embassy during the Shah era, and after the revolution, she was punished for having associated too much with Westerners. They fixed her nose."

December 26
ROUTE: TEHRAN—THE DESERT

Horrible night. I was alternately freezing and sweating. Went to the bathroom all the time. I eat Imodium and I leave Tehran on shaky legs, while the embassy staff waves Swedish flags. I get out into the desert. Behind me, the city is enveloped in a thick fog. It's getting hot. Still, I cycle in pants and a long-sleeved shirt, so as not to offend the Muslims.

Soon, I pass the construction site at Khomeini's grave. It's a long-term project. I drove by here three years ago, and the workers were digging in the same places then, too, just as they are now. My nausea is returning. I get a cold sweat and have to yank down my pants and relieve myself close to a couple of pine trees and within sight of the Ayatollah's tomb. Probably a capital offense.

December 28

ROUTE: QOM—KASHAN

I get a room in a hotel. I'm feverish and my eyes are bloodshot. My head hurts. My temples are pounding. I feel like I'm at 26,000 feet. I stagger out from the hotel, looking for a doctor, but everything in town is closed. It's a holiday. It's another holiday!

December 29

KASHAN

I get a penicillin shot at a small hospital.

New Year's Day

ROUTE: ARDESTAN—ARDAKAN

At midnight on New Year's Eve, I lie in the desert, close to an asphalt factory and some heaps of gravel. I look up at the sky and over to the horizon. I see no fireworks, no firecrackers, no joy, nothing.

January 5, 1996

ROUTE: AHMAD ABAD—KERMAN

A yellow Renault is parked by the road. When I pass it, a couple in their late twenties or early thirties appear. They wave for me to stop. I know what they want. During the last few days, it has happened perhaps fifty times. People invite me to their homes to ask me the truth about Western sins and joys. It's very kind of them, it really is. But—with all due respect—this country is driving me crazy. I can't stand saying nice things about mullahs and ayatollahs any longer. I need to get some sleep. I find a place to spend the night underneath a power-line pylon.

January 6

ROUTE: KERMAN—MAHAN

I sleep under the open sky. A full moon shines over the dry landscape. There are some tiny, twiggy bushes — the only plant that will grow here. Far away in the distance, I see high mountains. I encounter the yellow Renault again. First, I curse. I've been feeling like a circus animal these last few days. Everywhere, people honk their horns and shout:

"Hey, mister! You come here."

Then this time I think, "Okay, why not?" I should not be so quick to pass judgment on these people. In a way, I sympathize with them. There are no Westerners here. There is a ban on satellite dishes, and in the official propaganda, the Western world is depicted as a hellishly sinful place. Surely, people have an inherent, healthy curiosity. They realize that the propaganda is just that, and they want to know the truth. I don't want to flee like a scared stranger any longer. Actually, I've always been a very curious person, so I smile and accept their invitation. The name of the couple in the yellow Renault is Mahmood. They are very kind. They help me change money and extend my visa. Then there's the usual problem.

Before they can invite me to their home, they need a permit signed by a high-ranking official. We go to the police station in Kerman. The person in charge is not in. We wait for a long time, and finally I suggest we have lunch in a restaurant instead.

We leave. I cycle after the yellow Renault into a traffic circle, where a gray Jeep appears out of nowhere. The driver, a young man with a mustache, shouts at me. I try to steer clear of him, but he cuts me off anyway, and I ram into another car and crash on the pavement. People are staring at me. There are lots of cars and bikes around. Just a few seconds ago, they were all moving, but now all movement has stopped, and everyone wants to see what's going to happen next.

Anger surges within me. I run up to the Jeep, tear the door open, grab the driver, shake him, and shout furiously in English: "What are you doing?!"

Then something strange happens. The driver goes pale. He

looks both terrified and offended, as if I'd somehow humiliated him in a way that can't be remedied. It's almost eerie – but when the police and the mullahs arrive, he revs up his engine and speeds away.

A while later, back in the city of Kerman, I hear the sound of a motorcycle roar up behind me. The Mahmoods' yellow Renault guides the way in front of me. Along the roadside, people are selling their goods. A man pulls a fruit cart. Two veiled women dressed all in black walk by, and on a bench, a little boy leafs through a booklet. I still hear the loud motorcycle engine. I turn around; two men are on it. The one in front grips the handlebars; the one in back – the driver of the gray Jeep – holds a long wooden stick above his head, ready to strike me.

They zoom past, I duck, and the stick hits the back of my head with such force that the pole breaks. The motorcycle disappears down a side street. Out of the corner of my eye, I see the gray Jeep, full of angry men.

Lunch with the Mahmoods is a frustrating experience. I answer their questions, but I'm unfocused. I'm not really there.

"No," I say. "I have no kids."

"Yes, I do have a television."

January 7

ROUTE: MAHAN—BARAVAT

I pitch my tent next to a dried-up river bed. It rains during the night. At 7:00 A.M., the pain in my head wakes me up. I have a large bump where I got hit. It aches. I think about the man who hit me. I saw his face the moment before he struck me. He was weeping. He looked as if, at last, he was getting his revenge for a life full of injustices. Or did he believe he was fighting a religious battle – a jihad – against the powers of imperialism? I wish I could have heard the other side of the story: his story. Because while I write this, the Jeep driver is telling his friends something else.

But what?

January 10

ROUTE: ZAHEDAN—MIRJAVEH

I'm approaching the Pakistani border. There are watchtowers along the road. I get stopped by idle soldiers who want to poke fun at me.

"You Western people! Ha ha!"

A car full of soldiers drives past me at dusk. They look at me with clouded eyes; they have been smoking hashish.

"Mister, the light is too weak," one of them says, reaches out of the car window, and firmly grips my arm. "Problem!" he exclaims. They all nod, as if to underscore what a big problem we are talking about. I stop, and the soldiers explain that I have to spend the night in their barracks. For safety. When I answer that I'm planning to sleep under the open sky, they reply: "No, no. Very dangerous."

I don't know what could be so dangerous out in the waste-land, apart from the soldiers themselves. Still, they are dead set on saving me. Two of them hold onto my rear wheel, and later, after I manage to break free and have found a place to sleep next to a lamppost, I'm surrounded by soldiers smoking cigarettes who knock the ash on top of my sleeping bag, tear down my clothesline, and keep saying, as if repeating a mantra: "Very, very dangerous!"

January 13, Pakistan

ROUTE: NOK KUNDI—YAKMACH

I've biked 4,898 miles. All around me I see only sand. The silence is deafening. I think about that tough blond reporter from the tabloid *Expressen*. Perhaps I should give her something to think about.

Nothing is impossible.

January 17

DALBANDI

Fredrik and Renata are here to film me. We are close to the Afghan border now, but we hear that there are disturbances in Dalbandi, the town we are heading for.

"Dalbandi, problem? Bang, bang?" I ask a policeman, in an attempt to communicate.

"No," he says. "Dalbandi. Boom!" — as if a *boom* was much worse than a *bang*, which I suppose anybody who's read comic books already knows. We eventually learn that the people of Dalbandi are protesting because the authorities have broken their promise to bring electricity to the town. An isolated civil war has erupted, and when we pass by Dalbandi, we see burning tires and makeshift roadblocks made of boulders and old cars.

January 26

ROUTE: RAKHNI—SAKHI SARWAR

I struggle up an endless hill. The landscape is extremely barren, but at least there are a few thorny bushes and dried-up riverbeds that seem to have had water in them not too long ago. I meet men wrapped in beautiful shawls and turbans, and armed with the omnipresent Kalashnikovs.

When I reach the top of the hill, it's dusk. The sun sits on the horizon like a large orange, and the road winds away below it. It's very beautiful. I speed down the hill on the bicycle. I'm sweaty and tired. Then by chance I glance at the odometer and see that it reads 8,848 kilometers.

I'm spellbound by these numbers. At first I can't figure out what's so special about them. Then I realize that I have biked the number of kilometers equal to the height of Mount Everest in meters — and I'm exuberant. I let out a yell.

It's a sign, I think to myself, a sign.

January 31

ROUTE: SULEIMANKI—QAZUR

If I stop my bicycle, I am immediately surrounded by people. Yesterday, a man snatched my map out of my hands, and when I snatched it back, he grabbed my sweater — so I hit him, and he toppled over, groggy and frightened. Now my hand is swollen and I'm ashamed. Why has the atmosphere turned hostile again? Today, people grabbed at my rear wheel, and when I turned around, I saw that the wheel was broken. I am in a small village south of Lahore. I have cycled along roads lined with long rows of trees and past stinking lakes where carrion and black algae float. In the afternoon, I stop in the village to drink two Pepsis.

While I drink, the mood around me becomes more excited, and after a while people are shouting with joy, as if my broken wheel is a great victory for them. They begin throwing things at me, and soon hundreds of people are gathered, cheering each other on until they have reached what feels like a prelude to a lynching. I see a little repair shop, only a tin shed, and I roll my bike inside. I try to shut the door behind me, but at least ten people slip inside.

The mechanic greets me. He takes off my rear wheel and disappears with it. Outside, I can hear the madness mounting. People pound against the sheet-metal walls and throw stones at them until there is a roaring sound inside the shed which must reach close to seventy decibels. Then suddenly the lights go off. It is pitch black. The crowd cheers and shouts as if it were some damned soccer game. I get really worried. Where is my wheel? What will happen when I go back outside?

Fifteen minutes later, the mechanic returns. He nods his head gravely at me, as if to signal that he is the only sane person in a village full of madmen. In the midst of all the hysteria, he has fixed my rear wheel. I thank him, put the wheel back on the bike, and prepare myself to run the gauntlet.

With a crazed energy, I push my bike outside and pedal away as fast as I can while sticks, stones, and shoes fly at me. But before I am entirely out of danger, I have to throw one guy to the ground who won't get out of the way.

February 3

ROUTE: LAHORE—AMRITSAR

Distance covered: 5,938 miles

I weigh 181 pounds, which means I have lost 24 pounds since I left Sweden. I'm going to have to gain some weight if I want to make it to the summit of Everest. I pass by a Western couple, two hippies dressed in tie-dyed clothes and bracelets, but long gone to the dogs. They sit smoking pot while riding in a horse-drawn carriage, heading for India, I think. Between them sits a child perhaps two years old.

February 11

ROUTE: BABUGARH—MORADABAD

India is a paradise after Pakistan, and soon after passing the India-Pakistan border, I meet an exotic woman clad in beautiful shawls who spontaneously wishes me good luck on my journey. This makes me strangely happy. It's been a long time since I saw a woman. In eastern Turkey, Iran, and Pakistan, I saw only men, and now, when a woman on the street even smiles at me, the whole world looks better. The landscape is the same as in Pakistan, but still, so much more beautiful.

I pass between long rows of tall trees. The treetops almost touch each other, creating a roof over my head. It's like cycling through a long tunnel made of twigs and leaves. Sometimes, I see vultures sitting on carcasses that have been left on the roadside. It's hot, and the dead water buffalo inflate like balloons in the heat. When the vultures and the crows pick at them, their stomachs explode, revealing a stinking sludge.

I see many poor people, of course. I'll never forget the man who crept along the road with part of an empty can in his hand. He was tiny and desiccated, his leathery skin heavily furrowed and covered with dirt. His teeth were yellow, his arms bony. I've never seen a person who looked so utterly destitute. In India, people burn dried cow-dung patties to heat their homes. And this man was crawling on his knees, gathering the dung from the holy cows.

February 18

ROUTE: KHALILABAD—NUTWANA

I stop to pee. I look out over an apple orchard. Suddenly I feel a terrible pain in my lower body. When I look down, I see that I've stepped into a hole and that the air is full of hornets. I run, chased by a swarm of insects. I reach three clay huts, and when people see me, they throw leaves and grass on a fire and yell at me to stand in the smoke. So I stand in the smoke, and every time I try to step out of it, the hornets attack. They recognize me, those beasts, and for forty-five minutes, I can't leave the smoke. The villagers go and get my bike for me, and I jump up and pedal away in a panic.

After a mile or two, I stop. I'm dizzy. My body is pounding. I ache as if I've been hit with poisoned arrows. I'm close to a jungle. The forest is dark and thick. I see monkeys; an old lady chases one away that has stolen her bananas. The drama acts out like a comical sketch, and I think my tormented face cracks up in a smile.

I count the stingers as I pluck them out. There are close to thirty.

February 20

ROUTE: BAIJWALA—CHITAWAN (NEPAL)

Distance covered: 6,887 miles

The landscape is wonderful: woods, meadows, streams, grazing animals. The women are painfully beautiful. I'm close to my goal.

February 22

ROUTE: MALEKU—KATHMANDU

The bicycle, my old friend, is finally breaking down. First, I notice that the rear wheel is worn out. With a lot of work, I change the tire and the inner tube. I break several of my tools in the process. Then I get a flat tire on my trailer. Soon, my left pedal starts squeaking. The handlebars creak, and the gears and derailleur start to pack it in. Now I can use only the highest gear — and I'm in the mountains. It's getting dark. People call after me, but I don't answer. I'm in my own world, and I just want to get to Kathmandu and put an end to this misery. I struggle hard. Coming round a curve, I see a long, killer hill in front of me. Far away, I see two trucks, and even farther away, the top of the hill. Below me, a beautiful valley opens, but the road is dismal and the diesel fumes are thick.

I walk my bike. My sweat is pouring. Suddenly, I get a cramp in my right calf, and I mutter: "No! Nothing can stop me now. I'm going to get to Kathmandu, even if it means I have to carry the bike. I'll never give up!"

When I reach the hilltop, a feeble moon is shining, and in the distance, I see a range of high, snow-covered peaks. I look at them for a while, and then I lower my gaze to the valley floor spread out below me. Lights flicker in the quiet darkness.

"It's Kathmandu," I say to myself, and I feel my eyes tear up.

"I'm there. I've reached my first goal."

5

So MUCH WRITING HAS been done about climbing—and life—at the highest altitudes. In medical books, of course, but in mountaineering chronicles, too, describing how thin the line is that separates you from the great unknown when you're struggling at high altitude. Most high-altitude mountaineers—who of course are completely normal people at home—often have supernatural experiences in the mountains.

It is not entirely unexpected that the brain acts in funny ways up there. At 29,028 feet, the height of Everest, the amount of oxygen is only a third of that found at sea level. The jet stream winds can reach over 300 miles per hour, and in the dry atmosphere, a panting, hyperventilating climber loses precious body liquid with every breath. Even in a blizzard with temperatures of minus forty degrees Fahrenheit, at high altitude you still have to drink more water than you would in the Sahara—often two to three gallons a day.

On Everest, the sun burns without mercy, scorching your skin and making you snow-blind. Your blood pressure rises. The climber breathes four times as fast as he would at sea level to boost oxygen intake in the lungs, and the body produces extra red blood cells in order to carry as many oxygen molecules as possible to the heart, brain, and muscles.

"Mount Everest exists not only on the surface of the earth but in the landscape of the mind," journalist Claudia Glenn Dowling writes in *Life* magazine. "It is climbed on both planes, physical and mental."

As you ascend, your reality changes. Experiments show that climbers at 26,000 feet take fifty percent longer to understand a sentence than a six-year-old at sea level does. At high altitude, the power to reason becomes the first victim.

The lifeless desolation found on the mountain also affects a climber. The beauty of the landscape is magnificent, but many climbers also feel lonely and vulnerable. I was speaking with a fellow climber in Everest Base Camp whose colleague was sitting up on the mountain waiting to die. All hope for his friend was lost.

"Freezing to death is not the worst part," he told me. "The worst part is the loneliness on the mountain, to see darkness come and hear the gale howl."

Peter Habeler, who together with Reinhold Messner was the first person to scale Mount Everest without supplemental oxygen, wrote about the myths surrounding the mountain in an article entitled, "The Loneliest People in the World." According to one legend, the ghosts of dead climbers rove around the highest heights, helping us — the living — to reach the summit. Habeler claims he is no believer in ghost stories, but he has experienced, firsthand, how the imagination can conjure up strange things "in this lonely environment, which is so hostile to life. . . ."

The summit of Mount Everest is situated in the outer layers of the troposphere, and at the beginning of the stratosphere. When mountaineers attain the top of Everest, they don't just reach the highest point on earth, they pit themselves against the most arduous physiological test the human body can withstand. The height of Everest is such that it's just barely possible to scale the mountain without breathing supplemental bottled oxygen. "Were it 1,000 feet lower, it would have been climbed in 1924. Were it 1,000 feet higher, it would have been an engineering problem," the climber Peter Lloyd said. Above 28,500 feet, a human being stands in life's borderland. Peter Habeler, describing his first oxygenless ascent of Mount Everest on May 8, 1978, writes:

> We had obviously reached a point at which normal brain functions had broken down or at least were severely limited. Our attentiveness and concentration declined; our instinct no longer reacted as reliably as before; the capacity for clear logical thinking had also apparently been lost. I only thought in sensations and loose associations, and slowly I was overcome by the feeling that this threatening fearful mountain could, in fact, be a friend.
>
> Today I am certain that it is in these positive and friendly sensations that the real danger on Everest lies.

Many climbers have an almost religious reverence for the mountain, especially the Sherpas — and perhaps this, too, has something to do with their experiences at high altitude. If you live close to the mountains in the Himalaya, you develop a personal relationship to them. You start seeing them as moody entities — either friends or foes, I suppose, depending on the weather and the circumstances. Every mountain has its own peculiarities, and even if we can understand them to some degree, mountains remain essentially unpredictable. I know that I can communicate with the mountains. It's also equally essential that I listen to their advice and admonitions — and that I read the signs of encouragement or warnings both within myself and in nature. Because it is these subtle signs that most clearly show me as a mountaineer the dangers I must confront—and the best time to take action. I often ponder that I have to be sensitive and humble on the mountains. Overt pride and hubris are probably the most common causes of tragedy at high altitude, and to date, my strongest experience of this had been on my ascent—and bare survival—on K2.

When I arrived in Kathmandu, I wondered how Mount Everest would receive me, but additionally I wondered what kind of climbers were headed to Everest this season. I was the first "Everester" in town, and this suited me just fine. I got a room in a nice hotel, rested, and feasted on food and chocolate to build up the subcutaneous fat I'd need later on. I bought a few maps, books, and other things. I enjoyed being a tourist. I walked the streets, smiling and greeting people, while thinking about what lay ahead.

The city was the same as ever. Kathmandu is situated in the middle of the Himalaya at an altitude of 4,360 feet. There are innumerable Hindu and Buddhist temples, and small shops and craftsmen selling their wares line the streets. I felt at home here and was happy to revisit the Monkey Temple, a temple where wild monkeys run freely around a Buddhist stupa decorated with the giant all-seeing eyes of the Buddha.

Although it was the end of February, I knew Kathmandu would soon be full of climbers. The winter jet stream winds were still blasting the summit of Everest, making conditions impossible for climbing, but as the summer monsoon approached in early May, it would push the jet stream winds north, and the most favorable conditions of the year—the first two weeks of May—would ensue. So in Kathmandu in March each year, mountaineers from around the world gather to prepare their expeditions.

Another sign indicating the climbing season was approaching was the appearance of the Reuters journalist Elizabeth Hawley. Hawley is a furrowed, schoolmarmish original who has been writing about mountaineering from Kathmandu for thirty-three years. Nearly sixty years of age, she's short and gray-haired, and drives an old Volkswagen. She tracked me down on the third day after my arrival and informed me that eleven expeditions were permitted to climb Everest from the Nepalese side this season. It sounded like a lot of teams and a lot of people.

"The day after tomorrow," she said, "a South African expedition arrives. Nelson Mandela has given them his personal blessing. If they make it, it will be the first time a black person reaches the summit."

We talked about Benoit Chamoux, who had recently died on the mountain Kangchenjunga. Chamoux, famous for his record-breaking speed ascents, claimed he had scaled all the world's four-teen peaks over 8,000 meters — all except Kangchenjunga. But this wasn't true. In mountaineering circles, it was known that he turned around thirty vertical feet from the summit of Shisha Pangma.

"It's the same thing with Carlos," I said to Miss Hawley.

Carlos Carsolio was now headed for Manaslu, which he claimed would be his fourteenth — and last — 8,000-meter summit. But I knew that he was lying, too. David Sharman and I knew he never summitted on K2. We knew this because Carlos was part of the 1993 Slovenian K2 expedition, as were we — and that two hun-dred feet from the summit, they all turned around. Once they returned to Base Camp, they fabricated a lie saying that the expe-dition had reached the summit.

When I said this, Elizabeth Hawley's eyes darkened. She probably thought I was just being jealous. But why should I be? I had photos to prove that I climbed K2.

"It's a damned pity," I thought when she had left and I was alone in my hotel room. "There's bluffing in mountaineering, but no one wants to touch it. No one dares to. No one writes about it and makes it public. People prefer to accept these lies." As for myself, if I say I am climbing alone and unsupported — and I get a small amount of help from someone along the way—I openly admit to having been helped. The same goes for reaching a summit—or not reaching it. I tell the truth, I explain what happened.

One should never attack another climber's credibility based on loose suspicions, but you have a responsibility, I think, to mention the most blatant cases. The credibility of mountaineering depends on it. Once, I attended a talk given by two well-known Swedish climbers—I've decided not to name them here—who claimed that they had reached the summit of Broad Peak in Pakistan. But I had read in the magazines *Climbing* and *Mountain* that they hadn't. When I pointed this out, they were evasive.

"It's hard to know exactly where the summit is," they answered.

They knew as well as I did that that was a lie.

Later, a Swedish mountaineering magazine wrote: "The climbers didn't summit on Broad Peak. That's that."

Before then, these two climbers and I had seen each other sometimes. I then received a letter from them, saying something to the effect of: "We've heard you're one of those backbiting our expedition. Call us, and we'll talk about it."

I left a message on their answering machine, but then we lost touch. It might seem harsh, but you must have absolute and unconditional trust in your fellow climbers. Once you're on the mountain, each climber has responsibility for other people's lives, and if he lies about his conquests, he might lie about other essential things on the mountain, too—and bring on disaster. That's how I see it.

Unfortunately, even more so today, the high cost of mountaineering puts a lot of pressure on climbers. The debts can be heavy, before, during, and after an expedition, and to fail on the mountain means a dramatically decreased income from lectures and sponsors after you return home. Still, the general public ought to be impressed by those who admit that they turned around short of the summit, because that's a sign of mental strength. A good climber possesses the courage to turn back – even when the summit is within reach. He never forgets that the ascent, climbing up, is only half the trip. You have to get down, too, and most casualties in the mountains happen during the descent. The greatness of a climber is not measured by his or her ability to reach the summit on the first attempt. What matters most is your attitude, your will to not give up, to try again.

A couple of days later, I met the South African Everest team. I don't recall exactly when it was that I started worrying about them. The first member I met was the South African journalist Ken Vernon, but he didn't know anything about climbing anyway. Which wasn't very surprising, because ignorant reporters are not a rare phenomenon. Still, he was a great guy, and we agreed to work together to organize some filming from a helicopter and a few other things. Then the "proper members" of the expedition showed up, and it didn't take long before they were all talking about their leader, Ian Woodall. He was a sexist, they said, and "racist, power-crazy, a liar, and just generally a big bastard."

"And he embezzled money from our expedition."

"Did you know him from before?" I asked, stunned by their accusations.

"Not at all," they answered. It turned out that no one on the team knew anyone else.

The expedition included both black and white climbers. Of course, that was a big thing for South Africa. This, combined with the fact that no South African expedition had ever climbed Everest before, prompted Nelson Mandela to meet with the team before its departure. Thanks to this, it was easy for them to find sponsors, and they had a large budget. The main sponsor was the Johannesburg newspaper the *Sunday Times;* they were also backed by major South African companies.

Some members of the expedition had hardly seen snow or ice before. It could have been quite comical watching them slipping and sliding on the glacier—if climbing Mount Everest weren't such a serious business. The team did have three strong climbers, among them the star climber Andy de Klerk—but all three soon pulled out, in protest of the leader, Ian Woodall.

"You couldn't trust him," Andy de Klerk said to the writer Jon Krakauer. "We never knew if he was talking bullshit or telling the truth. We didn't want to put our lives in the hands of a guy like that."

It's amazing that Ian Woodall managed to become leader of an expedition charged with so much national prestige and significance. People said that the entire nation of South Africa backed the effort. The South African papers wrote about the expedition as if it were a national soccer team headed for a world championship. In spite of mounting problems in South Africa, there was still an exultant joy over the new government, and a national team going abroad to compete with other international teams was a great event. Mountaineering is not a competitive sport in the strictest sense, but triumphs on the mountains sometimes get as much attention as a World Cup soccer match. I believe that many people experience a sense of victory when their fellow countrymen scale a high peak or reach a remote, inaccessible place. You feel the communal joy of moving forward.

Woodall had taken the initiative to organize the expedition, and perhaps that alone explains how he could hold on to the leadership, even though his lies and threats soon caused a scandal in his home country. Woodall was white, thirty-nine years old, and a former army officer. He was loquacious. He liked to brag about his part in South Africa's brutal conflict with Angola in the 1980s, and claimed that he secretly had been far behind enemy lines. He also said he had scaled many 8,000-meter peaks in the Himalaya. He had led the command of the British Army's Long Range Mountain

Reconnaissance Unit, and been an instructor at the Royal Military Academy at Sandhurst, England.

None of this was true, as Jon Krakauer showed in his book *Into Thin Air*. Woodall never went behind enemy lines in the war against Angola, and as for climbing 8,000-meter peaks, Woodall had been a client on two expeditions to Nepal led by Scotsman and Everest veteran Mal Duff, one to 20,305-foot Imja Tse (better known as Island Peak), and the other to the fairly easy, 26,545-foot Annapurna. On both expeditions he failed to reach the summit. That was the sum of Woodall's Himalayan climbing experience. A "Long Range Mountain Reconnaissance Unit" simply didn't exist, and Woodall never was an instructor at Sandhurst. Also, he lied about who was on the Everest permit he acquired from the Nepalese Ministry of Tourism—but that's a whole story in itself.

Woodall keenly wanted to have a woman on the team. The candidates were to compete for the slot while training on Kilimanjaro (19,340 feet) in Tanzania. After two weeks, Woodall had shortlisted two women, Cathy O'Dowd and Deshun Deysel. Then he declared that since they were of equal ability, he would bring them both to Nepal.

But he would let only one of them climb on Everest. Which one, he would decide in due time. Cathy O'Dowd was white, Deshun Deysel black. The arrangement was so unbelievably stupid that the only reasonable explanation was that Woodall hoped that the rivalry between the two women would strengthen his own power. Not surprisingly, more problems arose. When the strong black climber Ed February left the team in protest, Deshun Deysel was the only black person left in the expedition.

In fact, Deysel—who had paid $35,000 to Woodall for her place—was now the one who legitimized the whole expedition. Apart from her, the group consisted of middle-class whites. But soon it was discovered that Deysel's name was not on the application for the Everest climbing permit. Either Woodall had never even contemplated letting Deysel climb, or he wanted to cause problems. To climb Everest without a permit can lead to huge fines.

As the press accounts in South Africa surrounding the expedition grew increasingly negative, Woodall threw out the reporter Ken Vernon and the photographer Richard Shorey, both of whom I had gotten to know and like. This was a surprising move, considering that their employer, the *Sunday Times*, was the expedition's main sponsor. When the editor of the *Sunday Times*, Ken Owen, pointed this out to Woodall, along with some other irregularities, Woodall threatened to kill Owen. He claims that Woodall told him: "I'm going to rip your —— head off and ram it up your ——."

Nelson Mandela even sent a message to Woodall, asking for a reconciliation, but the old army officer stubbornly refused. And relinquishing leadership of the expedition was, of course, out of the question.

"I'll stay," Woodall said, and the South Africans weren't the only ones who were worried.

All in all, there were quite a few climbers with questionable experience levels on Everest this year. Inexperienced climbers who are stingy with the truth are a constant source of worry, and we soon realized that Woodall wasn't the only problem member on his team. Others on the South African expedition, I thought, had doubtful qualifications—which was confirmed when one day we heard that the competition between Deysel and O'Dowd was going to be settled on Kala Pattar (a small hill, a so-called trekking peak), not far from Everest. The women were going to race each other up the mountain.

"The winner climbs Everest," Woodall said. "The loser goes home."

While the South Africans were involved in their intrigues, we heard rumors that a Taiwanese expedition was also on its way to Everest. The team had once been saved by a helicopter from an altitude of 17,200 feet on Denali (Mount McKinley) in Alaska. One member of the expedition had died, and two had been severely injured. Still, the leader of the expedition, Gau Ming-Ho (who went by the nickname Makalu, the name of a mountain close to Everest), had been shouting: "Victory, victory! We made the summit!" — as if nothing had happened.

Talking about the Taiwanese and South African expeditions, the star guide Rob Hall exclaimed: "With so many inexperienced people on the mountain, I think something tragic will happen before we get out of here." His prediction came true, but not in the way that he had expected.

Myself, I tried to stay out of these petty rivalries and concentrate on positive thinking. I would soon walk to the mountain; I was just waiting for Renata and Fredrik. Meanwhile, I got to see Mount Everest from above. Saab's new pride, the Saab 2000 airplane, made a show flight over the Himalaya, and I was invited as one of the VIP guests. Sitting in the craft, bumping up and down, I saw the mountains Gaurishankar, Menlungtse, and Cho Oyu, and then we reached Mount Everest.

It was a strange feeling. The mountain looked so imposing and majestic, even seen like this, and I tried to imagine myself at the summit, like a tiny, fragile speck — when, at that sublime moment, champagne corks flew out of bottles that hadn't been opened and stewardesses fell into the laps of the VIP guests, whose faces expressed more worry than excitement. We had hit some very serious turbulence. I won't say I wasn't affected, but I still got out my camcorder and managed to film while the plane was thrown back and forth. Everest wanted to show us its power.

On March 3, Renata arrived in Kathmandu, and the next day we celebrated. In fact, all of Nepal celebrated. It was Color Day, a celebration in memory of a distant military victory. People took to the streets with jugs and buckets full of paint and water. And they looked at everyone else walking by with trickery, waiting for the right target to come close enough. Some carried balloons full of paint, others specially prepared bicycle pumps. We didn't feel like taking part. The climb was too close, so we went to our room.

When we got there, we realized there was a crazy, noisy carnival going on outside. People were splashing water and paint on each other, screaming, shouting, and giggling. Renata and I looked at each other. The serious business would have to wait. We filled glasses and the wastebasket with water and threw it on people down below, especially on those who still were dry and seemed like they wanted to protect their clothes. Then there was a buzz in the air. Renata jerked back and cried out that something had stung her shoulder. She had thrown water on a power line and had gotten an electric shock—but when we saw she was okay, we went outside and joined the madness.

The next day, I began biking from Kathmandu to Jiri, where the road ends and the mountain landscape begins. This final stretch of road ran through jungle-like areas thick with shrubbery, rhododendron bushes—and leeches. During the whole trip, from Stockholm to Kathmandu, there had been no stretch as hard as this last one. It was extremely steep, and for two days, I had to walk the bicycle.

Renata went by car to Jiri. We met up again in the village and prepared to trek to Base Camp. Renata hired porters, but I was going to do something that no other mountaineer had ever done: I would carry all of my own equipment to Everest Base Camp by myself. Expeditions in the 1950s had made use of some 2,000 porters, and in 1953, when Hillary and Tenzing triumphed, they needed 30 extra porters just to carry the coins that the rest of the porters were paid with.

Today's expeditions have traces of the same colonial extravagance. The Swedish expedition that climbed Everest in 1990 flew in several planeloads of equipment to the airstrip at Lukla at 19,350 feet. Then they walked with hundreds of Sherpas to Base Camp. In

the book, *Drömmen om Everest (The Dream of Everest),* Calle
Froste writes:

> *Of course, one may have ethical objections to our flights. Some
> people may for instance consider it nobler and more natural for
> a climber to walk all the way. The reason why we still chose to
> fly is simple. We saved approximately ten days in each direc-
> tion. Furthermore, we avoided the risk of catching illnesses in
> the lower, more polluted, areas. . . . If we hadn't availed our-
> selves of the help of Sherpas and their yaks . . . we would prob-
> ably not have reached Base Camp until the spring of the
> following year.*

I saw it differently. If the goal of mountaineering was just
to save time and effort, then I would have been satisfied scaling
Everest with the Saab aircraft. But my goal was not just to cover
a certain distance in the shortest possible time; I wanted to
prove something. So I left my bicycle in Jiri, unloaded the bike
trailer and put on my 4,900-cubic-inch backpack, and on top of
that my 9,000-cubic-inch duffel bag. I put another 1,800-cubic-
inch fanny pack around my waist, and on top of it all, I tied the
ropes, tent poles, my sleeping pad, and the rest of my climbing
equipment.

And there I stood, with 143 pounds on my back, gazing
toward the mountain.

Afterward, I jotted down some notes on my laptop computer about how it felt and what happened to me in the next few
days. But technology stole my notes! My computer asked me a
question. "Do you want to replace this file?" I found the question
strange. I didn't realize that what the machine actually meant was,
"Do you want to replace your notes with absolutely nothing?" I hit
yes, and everything I'd written between Kathmandu and Lobuche

disappeared like a snowy mist blowing uphill in the wind. Poof! Up into computer Nirvana.

It really didn't matter, though, because I will never forget my realization of having all of those hills and valleys and ups and downs ahead of me. I just wanted to lie down. After I hoisted on my backpack, I felt as if the force of gravity had been tripled. I took two steps. I was stunned. "This can't be true," I thought. "My pack can't be this heavy. There must be a mistake somewhere." I took a deep breath and hoped that my load would get lighter if I just thought this through very carefully.

All around me, the local people were laughing out loud. A disheveled, snotty-nosed kid pointed his finger at me. "Look at that crazy lunatic!" was what he probably said, and I was inclined to agree.

Suddenly, I realized that no one had faith in me, not even Renata, even though she tried to be encouraging. Later, she told me that it was then, for the first time, that she saw the same doubt in my eyes that I saw in everybody else's.

But I would rather collapse than give up.

"It will work," I muttered and staggered thirty feet ahead, pushing for a bench a little farther away. "If I can just make it there, I've made a start," I thought and tried to forget that I had to climb to 13,000 feet, then descend to 6,500, climb again to 12,500, descend again—and only then make the final ascent to Everest Base Camp at 17,100 feet.

It started to rain. The thick vegetation got thinner, and now and then, I came to narrow suspension bridges over steep ravines. There were still trees and moss growing on the slopes, and I could still hear the calming ripple of brooks. I had a long way to go to reach the first glacier. Sometimes, I could walk several hundred yards in one stretch, but then I would topple over, and my body ached, and now and then I just lay on the ground, feeling like I was dead. But the landscape was beautiful, and I tried to enjoy it and think about something other than trying to make it to the next bench, the next crest. Renata, poor girl, tried politely to slow herself down to my pace, but humans aren't made to move that slowly. While I dragged myself forward like a snail, she walked back and forth, or she sat by the road, waiting for me to catch up. Thanks to this, she got to know the members of many of the other expeditions this year. They passed by us, staring at me in amazement. And I was soon named the Crazy Swede — the idiot who carried his whole damn camp on his back.

It took me twelve days to reach Namche Bazaar, the well-known Sherpa village situated at 11,286 feet on a steep, amphitheater-like hillside in the upper Khumbu Valley. A few hundred families live here, surrounded by the snow-covered peaks. In spite of its moderate size, the village is an important place on any climber's map of the world. Virtually every famous Everest expedition (approaching on the Nepalese side of the mountain) has passed through and described the town in its account. Namche Bazaar really is the capital of the Sherpa people, and the best porters and guides in the history of climbing hail from here.

Five hundred years ago, the Sherpa people, originally from eastern Tibet, entered parts of northern Nepal and settled in the valleys south and west of the world's tallest mountain. They farmed and grew their main crop, potatoes, which the British had brought to India in the 1850s. Fortunately, potatoes can be successfully grown at over 14,000 feet. Today, the Sherpas still do a lot of heavy manual work and hauling, in addition to their work carrying loads for mountaineering expeditions because there are no roads here. And many people live above the tree line, so all the firewood needed for heating their homes has to be carried uphill, too. The nights are often cold; subzero temperatures are not uncommon.

In spring, many of the Sherpa villagers live off the climbing industry. More than 10,000 Westerners come annually to the Khumbu Valley, and many of the men in the local population work

as porters for eight or nine dollars a day. The trekking and climbing industry—which seems to grow only larger after each fatal
accident—also uses up a lot of firewood. As a result, the lowland
woods down-valley have thinned out, which has led to serious soil
erosion, crop failure, and landslides. These are yet other reasons to
make your way up the mountain with as little outside help as possible. Trekkers and climbers must be economical with natural
resources and not just march in with hundreds of hired hands.

By Western standards, the Sherpa people are generally poor
and uneducated. In Nepal, however, because of their strong (and
cheerful!) work ethic, they are among the wealthiest ethnic groups.
Most Sherpas are Tibetan Buddhists and would rather turn to
their lamas, their raisers of spirits, than consult a physician. Their
devout lives are guided by deeply held religious beliefs, and Bud-
dhism has long since merged with the Sherpas' reverence for
Mount Everest.

Many Sherpas believe that even reading a girlie magazine on
the mountain is an offense to Everest. Climbers or trekkers who
don't understand the religious meaning of the Khumbu mountains get into trouble with the locals. In Khumbu, everybody has
friends and relatives who have died in the mountains, on expeditions, and many Sherpas connect these deaths to the Westerners'
lack of respect for the Goddess Mother of the World—Mount
Everest.

Renata and I got a room in a small hotel on the slope of
Namche Bazaar. The room they gave us had a woodstove and two
stalls to sleep in. It turned out that American mountain guide
Scott Fischer's Mountain Madness Everest expedition was staying
at the same hotel, and as we sat in the hotel dining room, we saw
her for the first time. She entered like a queen. Dressed in tights
and wearing a scarf and a smart little hat covering part of her dark
hair, she seemed to be in her mid-thirties, was fit, and was quite
good-looking. But Renata got the feeling that this woman acted as

if we didn't exist. Suddenly she sat down and set up her satellite phone right in front of us! We had a satellite phone, too, so we knew it emits dangerous radiation. We moved away, but she didn't acknowledge us at all.

"Who's that?" we asked.

"Sandy Pittman," said a guy from the IMAX film team, who was in the Himalaya to shoot a giant-screen Everest documentary. "She's made of money. Bianca Jagger and Calvin Klein came to her farewell party. She's probably just phoning in another chapter of her journal to NBC's Web site."

Ms. Pittman was in the process of divorcing Bob Pittman, a producer and a cofounder of MTV. Rumor had it—but of course rumors are always simplifications—that Bob left her because she loved mountaineering more than she loved him. Six years prior, in 1990, Bob and Sandy had posed on the cover of *New York* magazine under the headline "The Couple of the Minute." It was said that they flew their own helicopter between their manor in Connecticut and their apartment on Central Park West in Manhattan, an apartment full of modern art and uniformed servants.

The farm in Connecticut was Bob's gift to Sandy for her thirtieth birthday. Ms. Pittman had a barn silo turned into a climbing wall; she even had three Sherpas living in a little house close to the mansion. Then she announced that she wanted to become the first American woman to climb the Seven Summits— the tallest peak on each of the seven continents—a concept first promoted and accomplished by another multimillionaire moun- taineer, the Texas coal and oil tycoon Dick Bass.

Along with the Norwegian shipping magnate/climber Arne Naess—who scaled Mount Everest in 1985, then months later mar- ried singer Diana Ross—Bass was the first of the superrich climb- ers. After he had conquered his seven peaks in 1985—with the aid of professional mountain guides and several famous mountaineering veterans—Bass wrote a bestseller, *Seven Summits*. When Pittman declared that she was not only going to repeat this conquest, but write a book of her own, she attracted plenty of media attention and even posed in climbing gear for *Vogue*. But Everest had already eluded her twice, even though she'd had the help of America's best mountain guides. The Sherpas especially remembered her 1993 Everest attempt when she showed up at Khumbu Base Camp with her nine-year-old son, Bo, and a nanny.

Sandy Hill Pittman, however, did not succeed in becoming the first American woman to conquer the Seven Summits. Forty-seven-year-old Dolly Lefever beat her to it. Still, Sandy chose to invest in a third Everest attempt. NBC sponsored her, and she in return was to file progress reports to their Web site—NBC Interactive Media—all the way to the top. One of her first postings on the Web soon became a classic in mountaineering circles. Before leaving for Nepal, Pittman wrote: "I wouldn't dream of leaving town without an ample supply of Dean & DeLuca's Near East blend and my espresso maker." Certainly no one else headed for Everest generated as much gossip as Pittman, and obviously not everything said about her was true. But it's a fact that she let the jeweler Barry Kieselstein-Cord make an expensive necklace for her that she intended to bury at the summit of Mount Everest—if she got there.

Pittman was a member of Scott Fischer's Mountain Madness Everest expedition. Along with New Zealand mountain guide Rob Hall, Fischer was the most respected guide on Everest, and the only one, besides Hall, who charged his clients $65,000 for a place on the team. But the clients saw it as a good deal. Scott Fischer's name seemed to vouch for safety and success—even though he had never actually guided on Mount Everest before, and had led only one commercial expedition to an 8,000-er, Broad Peak, in 1995. But, as a climber, Fischer had now secured an exceptional reputation. It hadn't always been that way.

Fischer was forty. He came from Seattle and had been married to Jeannie Price for fifteen years. Together they had two kids,

Andy, nine, and Katie Rose, five. He had loved the mountains ever since he was a kid, and while still a teenager, he taught climbing at the National Outdoor Leadership School—NOLS—in the Wind River Mountains of Wyoming.

"I fell in love with a climber," Jeannie Price later told *Life*. "To ask him to stop would be like asking him not to breathe."

Scott was known for being an almost obsessed mountaineer—like me—and his early expeditions were reputedly risky and extremely demanding, which was not necessarily good for his reputation, especially when he had a string of accidents.

His climbing partner, Don Peterson, said that Scott, when necessary, pushed himself beyond all limits of exhaustion. He became known for his astounding willpower. It didn't matter how much pain he was in; Scott would ignore it and press on.

Even though he made a series of impressive climbs in the 1980s, it continued to be hard for him to find sponsors. Financial problems plagued him. Then his wife, whom he had met at the age of eighteen, became a well-paid airline captain with Alaska Airlines, and thanks to her income, Scott began climbing full-time. He even founded his adventure-travel company, Mountain Madness. In the 1990s, things finally began to change, and Scott's daredevil reputation was replaced by one that commanded respect.

By many, though, he was still seen as the hippie of the business. He'd often smoke a joint or drink whiskey, but in 1994 he scaled Mount Everest without using supplemental oxygen. The expedition he belonged to also cleaned the mountain of some 2.5 tons of trash. After this, Fischer was in great demand. He began to lead fund-raising climbs for charities. On Kilimanjaro in Africa, he raised $500,000 for CARE, and on Alaska's Mount McKinley, he gathered funds for an AIDS charity.

Still, he hadn't made much money for himself. And when Scott heard how much Rob Hall earned as an Everest guide, he decided to use his own name to give the New Zealander some competition. If he succeeded, he'd be rich, comparatively, and that would be great — not because money meant that much to him, but because it would give him the opportunity to go on his own expeditions, on his own personal climbs, which was really where his heart was. With the help of his business partner, Karen Dickinson, he began attracting wealthy amateur climbers like Sandy Hill Pittman. And he found that for many people, $65,000 wasn't much money to spend for making their Everest dreams come true.

In 1996, Scott had eight clients, the same number as Rob. This one expedition would net him a few hundred thousand dollars. But climbing so much had put a strain on Scott and his family. He admitted that he didn't see his kids as much as he would like to, and his marriage was not uncomplicated. Scott had charisma; he attracted women. I first met him in Namche Bazaar.

We were sitting in the hotel's dining area. A group of Americans sat laughing while a Sherpa woman quietly waited on us. Below lay the valley with its snug stone and wood houses, green patches of shrubbery, and, above, the white rocks of neighboring peak Kwangde Ri. Out in the hotel yard, two boys played with a ball. Then everybody's head turned. A man with strong features and long blond hair tied back in a ponytail entered the room. Later, one of Scott's clients told *Life:* "Scott looked like a movie star, but movie stars become famous pretending to be someone like him." Well, he sure looked cool, and as he approached us, the Americans stopped laughing and greeted him respectfully. Scott sat down at their table, then after a while he came up to us. Scott was always very friendly.

"Hello, Göran!" he said. "Cool thing you've done. If I were fifteen years younger, I would do the same thing. I am getting old, you know."

I liked Scott Fischer from the start. I felt I could depend on him, and that evening I felt the beginning of a friendship. The next day Scott and his team headed for the Khumbu Glacier and Everest Base Camp, while I set off toward Lobuche Peak. My plan was to get acclimatized to the higher altitudes—the 20,000-foot level— somewhere other than the most dangerous place on Everest: the Icefall. Lobuche was known as a challenging "trekking peak," and on it I could climb to 20,075 feet and let my body get used to the altitude.

After a day's march from Namche Bazaar, you arrive at the famed monastery of Tengboche, a holy place for all Sherpas. The monastery, situated atop a green hillock at an altitude of 12,687 feet, is flanked by the mountains Kang Taiga and Ama Dablam. The IMAX team with their star filmmaker, the well-known and respected American mountaineer David Breashears, was already there to shoot a film sequence. My filmmaker, Fredrik Blomqvist, was there, too. The Buddhist monks perform their rituals only at specific times throughout the year—but they're not so orthodox that the schedule can't be altered in exchange for a large financial donation. So the ceremony was performed, and when Fredrik said that he wanted to shoot, too, Breashears replied curtly: "We're paying; you're not."

David Breashears is a big name, in both climbing and filmmaking. He shot the coolest episodes with Sylvester Stallone in *Cliffhanger,* a Hollywood mountaineering drama. Breashears has filmed mountains in China, Nepal, India, Pakistan, Russia, and Africa, and has received five Emmy Awards. He first came to Mount Everest in 1983, and soon he became the first American to climb Everest twice. In all, he's been on more than fifteen expeditions to the Himalaya, and in 1986, he made the classic documentary *Everest: The Mystery of Mallory and Irvine.* Now, ten years later, he was at work on his biggest project ever.

Although we initially saw the whole IMAX film team as being composed of rather supercilious people with unlimited financial resources, we soon became good friends. Thinking back on the episode with the monks in the monastery, it was really an example, I think, of the stark professionalism you have to adopt in the movie business. In any case, I passed through Tengboche and began my training climb, up Lobuche Peak.

At 19,000 feet — I checked the altitude on the altimeter watch on my wrist — I was struck by a severe headache. It wasn't dangerous but rather was a sign that my body was acclimatizing to the thin air. On April 9, I stood on Lobuche's fore-summit. Nuptse, Maleku, and Everest smiled at me in the morning sun, and the Sherpa village below looked like a warped chessboard. I continued climbing toward Lobuche's main peak, then reached a nasty, narrow snow ridge, which I straddled with each leg. Suddenly the right side of the ridge collapsed, but luckily I held on to the very thin left side.

"Damn!" I thought. "It's Everest I'm going for, not Lobuche."

So I turned back and climbed down. Even though I hadn't reached the main summit, I still felt energized and happy about my warm-up climb.

Two days later, after breakfasting in the village, I was reminded how small the mountaineering world is. Here came Davo, a crazy guy whom I met on K2 in 1993. He had tried to slalom ski down K2. He was dead serious about it, too, but fortunately he lost his skis in an avalanche. The very next year, he and his brother succeeded in skiing down Annapurna (26,545 feet) all the way to Base Camp without stopping once.

"This year," Davo said, "I'm going to get up on Everest, then ski down on the Tibetan side, past the Great Couloir, down to the foot of the mountain." Everest's Great Couloir is a giant, steep-sided gully down the mountain's North Face. Part of it is always in shade. It's like a deep well, collecting snow, and ripe for avalanches; another perfectly impossible "first."

Records of all sorts have been set on Everest: the highest hang-gliding, the most rapid ascent, the oldest summiteer and the youngest, the first Norwegian, first Russian, Swede, Spaniard, the first American woman, and then me; I wanted to be the first human who made it all the way from home to the top of the mountain under my own power. May the mountain gods be with me! Many people thought Mount Everest would lose its allure when Hillary and Tenzing reached the summit on May 29, 1953. But new challenges are created all the time by those of us who mourn that we weren't born earlier, when there were more records to set. I believe there is something deeply human in the drive to do what no one else has done before, to test the limit of what is considered possible, even if it's seen as insane by those who prefer peace and safety.

While I talked with Davo, another familiar face appeared. "Stiepe!"

"Göran!" he shouted back. Stiepe was the snow-blind Slovenian I had helped descend to K2 Base Camp. Today we didn't talk about the summit lie the Slovenians had fabricated; we were just genuinely happy to see each other.

"Did you know Zvonko keeps on fighting?" said Stiepe. "After the K2 drama he lost all his fingers down to the second joint, and all ten toes, too. But this year he's trying to find a new route up Ama Dablam. We climbers never give up, do we?"

We certainly do not give up; I made two trips carrying all of my gear and food from Namche Bazaar up to the Khumbu Glacier and, finally, Everest Base Camp. The final leg of the trek began with a long slope. Soon I saw Pumori, which flanks Base Camp to the left, or west. Rising on the opposite side of the glacier was Nuptse. The landscape was dry and barren; occasionally I passed a bush. There were also many yaks and Sherpas on the trail, and every so often, Buddhist prayer stones called a mani wall. Religious tradition says you must always walk around a sacred Buddhist object (a prayer wall, chorten, stupa, or temple) clockwise—always on the left. And you can be sure that I did! To pass to their right, counter-clockwise, brings bad luck and vexes the mountain gods; I was not taking any risks now.

Finally, I reached the Khumbu Glacier. I continued walking over the many loose stones and between large towers of ice, carrying my giant backpack. Other than some lichen on the rocks, the landscape was devoid of life. Sometimes on top of the glacial ice there was only a layer of gravel. I slipped.

"No! No injuries now. If I get hurt then I will break down."

I started again and walked as carefully as I could, as if I was crossing a minefield. At a glacial lake, I was forced to make a long detour. Then finally, at the top of yet another slope, I saw in the distance spots of color, dreamlike. After six months of continuous traveling, I had reached the multicolored nylon tent outpost of Everest Khumbu Base Camp sprawled across the mounds of loose, stony moraine. Generators hummed. And among the prayer flags, tents of all shapes, sizes, and colors, and mounds of stones, I saw familiar faces and South African, American, Taiwanese, and various Yugoslavian flags flapping in the wind.

I had arrived.

6

HOW AND WHEN DID THE story of Earth's highest mountain begin? In a way it started in 1808 when the British launched the Great Trigonometric Survey of India. The goal was to map the entire Indian subcontinent. After a time, the surveyors came to suspect that the volcano Chimborazo in South America—where many years later I surfed on a sliding snowfield in an avalanche—was not the tallest mountain in the world, as was believed in the seventeenth and eighteenth centuries. The place where the earth was closest to Heaven was rather in the Himalaya, in the kingdom of Nepal.

To measure the height of mountains, the surveyors used instruments called theodolites, which were so heavy and large that you needed twelve men to carry them. Training their theodolites on the distant peaks, they compensated for the refraction of light through the atmosphere, recorded their data, and slowly calculated the altitude of the Himalayan peaks.

In 1847, John Armstrong noted a peak which he called "b." He wrote that it seemed taller than Kangchenjunga, which up until then was believed to be the tallest peak in the range. The mountain was soon renamed Peak XV, but not until 1856 did the British Surveyor General of India Andrew Waugh declare that Peak XV was in fact higher than any other mountain measured in India.

But what was the mountain to be called? The survey was forward-thinking and retained local names for peaks whenever one could be ascertained. Thus Dhaulagiri, the White Mountain, and Kangchenjunga, the Five Treasure-Houses of the Snows, had kept their original names. But Andrew Waugh claimed that there was no obvious name for Peak XV. There were, it turned out, several existing local names. For centuries, the mountain had been called Chomolungma, the Goddess Mother of the World, by the Tibetan and Sherpa peoples. The Nepalese call it Sagarmatha. And there were several additional names, though none as well known and widely used as Chomolungma. Not only did this name express the reverence the native population had for the mountain, it also indicated that the people had divined that this was, in fact, the world's tallest mountain. The name Chomolungma had actually even been used on a Western map, published in Paris in 1733, but Andrew Waugh insisted that the mountain be named after his predecessor, the first Surveyor General of India, Sir George Everest.

The irony is that George Everest disliked honors, and it was he who had fought to preserve the original native names of the mountains. He objected vigorously to Waugh's proposal, but in vain. In 1865, one year before his death, Sir George Everest reluctantly agreed to give his name to the peak. It didn't take long before British mountaineer Clinton Dent declared that Everest ought to be scaled. He compared such an undertaking to the polar expeditions, which fascinated the world at that time. He was proven right; the dream of Mount Everest soon enchanted humanity.

But political problems made it difficult to enter Tibet and Nepal, and then came the First World War, so the first expedition to Mount Everest didn't get under way until the spring of 1921. One of the team members was George Mallory, a charismatic man with a literary bent. After serving in the war, he had become a headmaster but found school life petty. Mallory's salvation was mountain climbing, and he was the first Westerner to see Mount Everest in all its greatness.

"We're just about to walk off the map," he wrote in June 1921, signaling that he and his colleagues were heading into uncharted territory. He was fifty miles from Everest, on the mountain's northern, Tibetan side. For months, Mallory and the rest of the expedition had been approaching the mountain on foot, heading north through Sikkim onto the Tibetan plateau, then west toward the Everest region. Now they entered a grandiose landscape of limestone rocks and deep ravines. The sky was covered with monsoon clouds, and George Mallory could only guess where Everest was. He wrote:

> We gazed at [the cloudbanks] intently through field glasses as though by some miracle we might pierce the veil. Presently the miracle happened. We caught the gleam of snow behind the grey mist. A whole group of mountains began to appear in gigantic fragments. Mountain shapes are often fantastic seen through a mist; these were like the wildest creation of a dream. . . . Gradually, very gradually, we saw the great mountain sides and glaciers and arêtes, now one fragment now another through the floating rifts, until far higher in the sky than imagination had dared to suggest the white summit of Everest appeared.

I can sense what Mallory felt. It must have been an immense experience. When I first caught sight of Mount Everest after six months of traveling, I wept. I was standing on a narrow mountain path with my giant backpack. Below me lay a deep valley, and I muttered to myself: "There she is. There she is." I envy Mallory and his colleagues, who were the first to find a way up the mountain, those pioneers who walked on virgin ground and left the first human footsteps on the north side of the massif. Nowadays, there's precious little untrodden ground on Chomolungma.

George Mallory became the most fascinating and mysterious personage in the history of Everest. Originally, he climbed without supplemental oxygen because back then oxygen required much too heavy a device. "When I think of mountaineering with four cylinders of oxygen on one's back and a mask over one's face — well, it loses its charm," he wrote in 1922. But two years later, when setting out for the summit with his young colleague Andrew Irvine, he decided to use bottled oxygen. Perhaps it was a fatal mistake. "We'll probably go on two cylinders — but it's a bloody load for climbing," he wrote in his last surviving note.

He and Irvine were nearing the top. Far below, their colleague Noel Odell saw them as two black dots; then they disappeared from view. Irvine and Mallory were never again seen alive. On May 1, 1999, American researchers found Mallory's body at 27,000 feet on Everest's North Ridge. Many people want to believe that the pair actually reached the summit — twenty-nine years before Hillary and Tenzing. Most likely, they didn't, but it's a beautiful myth. Mallory and his partner Irvine were the first Westerners to die on Mount Everest. As of 1999, the mountain has claimed some 160 lives.

In 1935, and then again after World War II, in the early 1950s, British mountain pioneer Eric Shipton came to Everest. He recruited the gangly New Zealander Edmund Hillary and the powerful Sherpa Tenzing Norgay, whose son I would later meet at a critical moment. Eric Shipton and his expedition took pictures of a series of giant footprints in the snow on the mountain. On December 6, 1951, an image of a thirteen-inch footprint with a large outer toe and a well-defined heel was published in the *Times* under the headline: FOOTPRINTS OF THE 'ABOMINABLE SNOWMAN.'

According to legend, a creature part human and part beast lives in the Tibetan mountains. It is called the Yeti or the Abominable Snowman, and just like Scotland's Loch Ness monster, the creature has been captured in blurry and doubtful photographs (and in a couple of funny episodes in the comic book *Tintin*). The evidence Shipton discovered in 1951 was compelling, but the Natural History Museum in London suggested that the footsteps came from a giant monkey. Other authorities speculated on a new species that was a cross between an ape and a bear.

It's a fact, however, that Eric Shipton had a mischievous sense of humor. Some claimed that Shipton privately admitted to having embellished the footprints of a goat or another animal, turning them into something scary and prehistoric. Many years later, in Kathmandu, Fredrik Blomqvist and I were tempted to do something along the same line. We decided to make giant feet out of plywood, strap them to our boots, and go walking on the slopes. It would be a pity, we thought, if the myth of the Snowman died out. But we never carried out our plan.

In any case, Eric Shipton was replaced (with a certain amount of controversy) by John Hunt as the leader of the 1953 British Mount Everest expedition. On the morning of May 29, 1953, Hunt waited nervously for news from his climbers Hillary and Tenzing. Seen from the foot of the mountain, the weather around the summit seemed clear and calm. Actually, the wind was blowing hard, and when Edmund Hillary took off his goggles, he was temporarily blinded by the fine snow.

To Hillary's surprise, he was enjoying the climb. It wasn't until just below the South Summit that the situation turned critical. Here the snow became very soft, and if either man fell, the other wouldn't be able to arrest the fall with his axe. There was also some risk that they might set off an avalanche. "My solar plexus was tight with fear," Hillary recounted.

Tenzing climbed up to Hillary. Having donned their goggles and oxygen masks, the pair resembled science fiction characters. Hillary asked Tenzing for his opinion.

"Very bad, very dangerous!" replied Tenzing.

"Do you think we should we go on?"

"Just as you wish."

They kept climbing and reached firmer snow, but now they were getting tired. They reached the base of a rock cliff that later climbers called the Hillary Step. Exerting all their energy, they climbed the forty-foot vertical outcrop, then lay in the snow, panting and exhausted. But there was no turning back. They continued climbing, but they still couldn't see the summit, and Hillary wondered if he had the power to go on. But suddenly the ridge they were climbing began sloping downward; they could gaze out over the rocky Tibetan landscape to the north. Hillary later wrote:

"My first sensation was one of relief—relief that the long grind was over; that the summit had been reached before our oxygen supplies had dropped to a critical level. . . ." But there was not just relief. Hillary goes on: "I was too tired and too conscious of the long way down to safety really to feel any great elation." It took some time before "a quiet glow of satisfaction" spread within him.

In a typically correct Anglo-Saxon fashion, Hillary extended his right hand to Tenzing—who hugged him back. The men stood there for a few moments, embracing at the highest point in the world, as if to protect each other from the cold.

Edmund Hillary then took a sequence of pictures of his companion. He stands in a dark blue down jacket, holding his ice axe above his head, his face completely covered by the oxygen mask. His left leg is bent, as if he is stretching, and above him, the sky is black. Around his boots, there's a faint mist of snow. The picture has become a classic. Interestingly, no photographs were taken of Hillary on top. "Tenzing didn't know how to use a camera—and it wasn't the place to teach him," Hillary once explained.

Tenzing dug a hole and put a piece of chocolate in it, as an offering to the mountain god. In the same hole, Hillary placed a crucifix that John Hunt had given him for that purpose. Those were the first objects left at the summit of Everest. In the decades to come, there would be a lot more.

No one else on the expedition knew Hillary and Tenzing's fate. There was no radio contact, and the visual signal they'd agreed on making was made impossible by cloud banks and an oncoming storm. It was not until the next day that the victorious summiteers met their friends at Camp Four. As soon as James Morris, correspondent for the *Times,* heard the news, he descended to Base Camp and sent a coded message with a runner to Namche Bazaar. The message was telegraphed via Kathmandu to London, and three days later, on the morning of Queen Elizabeth's coronation, the newspapers blasted out the news of the conquest of the "Third Pole." The attention was unbelievable. Edmund Hillary was knighted; Tenzing Norgay became a national hero throughout Asia. In the 1950s, news that Everest had been scaled was as big as when Neil Armstrong first set foot on the moon.

Since then, thousands of people have invested enormous sums of money and risked their lives to scale Mount Everest. Many of them have contented themselves with repeating what Hillary and Tenzing did—which, of course, is impossible. Hillary and Tenzing were the first to ascend their route completely to the summit. They accomplished a feat that was still unknown. Since 1985 many have been satisfied to be ushered to the top by guides. But there are also those few who have found new routes up the mountain, up the north, west, and east sides, and new, more challenging ways in which to climb it. Most impressive was Reinhold Messner's feat when he scaled Mount Everest on August 20, 1980, totally alone and without using bottled oxygen. It was Messner and the mountain, period.

"At first there is no relief," he later wrote. "I am leached, completely empty. In this emptiness nevertheless something like energy accumulates. . . . I have climbed myself to a standstill, now I am experiencing regeneration, a return flow of energy."

The first time Messner and Peter Habeler scaled Everest without supplemental oxygen, in 1978, many people doubted it was true. A rumor spread that they had secretly breathed small doses of bottled oxygen. None were more suspicious than the Sherpas in the Khumbu Valley. They didn't want to believe that it was possible to scale the mountain in a natural way, when not even they, the people of the mountains, could do so. Reinhold Messner's triumph in 1980 was the final evidence that humans could indeed attain Everest's summit without breathing supplemental oxygen.

As I've said before, I wanted to go one step further. I wanted do absolutely everything by myself, from start to finish, from my home in Sweden to the summit. When I arrived at Base Camp, there were lots of people and lots of resources there, but as far as it was possible, I still wanted to act as if I were completely alone on the mountain. I ate only the freeze-dried food that I had hauled on my bike from Sweden, then I backpacked up to Base Camp. I didn't let anybody wait on me, even though Renata, Fredrik, my accountant, Torbjörn, and Magnus "Julle" Roman lived right next to me, with their own cooks and Sherpas.

Julle's job was to photograph me at the summit from an airplane. It wasn't cheap, and although some may think this doesn't blend well with my desire to do everything single-handedly, the pictures wouldn't help me climb. But I wanted them as definitive proof that I had reached the summit. I didn't want to be accused of lying. But, believe it or not, I also did not experience much pressure to succeed. All the phone calls I had received before I left home clearly showed me that most people did not think I would reach the top. And this knowledge imparted a feeling of peace. Now I had everything to gain.

I enjoyed life in Base Camp. I met old friends and made new ones, plus there were many funny characters. We lived between the

Scotsman Mike Trueman, who belonged to Mal Duff's expedition, and a group of soldiers from Serbia and Macedonia. Base Camp gossip said that the soldiers were war criminals on the run who'd taken refuge here at the end of the world. Or, they'd been declared too crazy to fight—and had been exiled to Mount Everest. In any case, they certainly knew how to party, as did Mike. Several times a day, he staggered past our tents.

"There's nothing worse than getting sober again in the afternoon," he'd blurt, drunk out of his mind, dressed in shorts. The cold didn't bother him. Mike was unkempt, slovenly in his habits, and talked with a thick Scottish accent that was unintelligible even when he was sober. I thought he was cool, with his beard and long, dark hair. The guy didn't care what anybody thought of him, and he and the soldiers often sat together, singing.

One day Renata walked by their tents. She was looking for Charlotte Noble, a strange South African woman who usually hung out with us but today was nowhere to be found. It was after dark, and the tent where the soldiers lived was roaring; they were having a party. Renata cautiously unzipped the tent door and peeked in. Fifteen men sat inside. In front of them, on the tent floor, were bottles, ashtrays, other trash, and a pack of cards spread out. All the men beamed giant smiles to her.

"Good evening!" Renata said in fluent Czech. "Have you seen Charlotte?"

The men roared, almost in unison: "Come on in! Have a beer!"

They were suffering from a shortage of females, and a beautiful young woman like Renata no doubt appeared as an angelic vision to them. But Renata was not as interested as they. "Thank you," she said and left.

Women who did want to find romance in Base Camp had no problem. There was, for instance, one woman whose husband had died the year before on the neighboring mountain Pumori.

Her journey here was part of her mourning process. She was not the first woman to journey to the Himalaya on such a mission. After their loved ones—Peter Boardman and Joe Tasker—disappeared attempting the first ascent of Everest's Northeast Ridge, in the autumn of 1982, Hillary Boardman and Maria Coffey came to Everest to try to reconcile themselves with their deaths. Coffey wrote afterward that when she left the mountain, she felt "calm, almost happy. . . . It was a fine place to spend eternity."

The woman who was seeking solace for her grief this time— I forget her name—found another kind, too. The blond, superman Russian climber Anatoli Boukreev appeared. The woman soon shared his tent and left it feeling invigorated every morning, which worried the Sherpas.

Boukreev was one of Scott Fischer's two assistant guides. The other was Neal Beidleman. Boukreev was considered strong and technically skilled, but he came from another climbing tradition than did Fischer and—especially—Rob Hall.

Scott and Rob had, to put it cynically, some clients who'd done most of their climbing on the StairMaster or on the spiral staircases in their office buildings or duplex apartments. Some of them probably were also used to getting as high as mountaintops at cocktail parties. Rob and Scott became their daddies on the mountain; they'd been paid to. Anatoli, on the other hand, came from an Eastern European climbing tradition where the mountain guides were simply guides, not baby-sitters.

"If a client can't make it without a lot of help from the guide, then he shouldn't be here," Anatoli said.

Scott thought Anatoli was nonchalant toward the clients. He had paid him $25,000 to be his assistant guide, and he thought he had the right to expect more from the Russian. As a result, there was a certain amount of tension between them.

Then there were the South Africans. They built a low wall of stones around their camp, turning it into a psychiatric ward—at least that's how we put it when we talked about them. Peripherally, I got involved in the South African drama after I gave a tent to the journalists whom the expedition leader, Ian Woodall, threw out. And I also helped the South African climbers who were sliding around on the ice. They had no expertise in snow and ice climbing. One of them didn't even know how to strap his ice axe to his backpack. Another fell on the ice and was rendered unconscious. All in all, the South Africans were a sad farce.

Everest Base Camp was indeed a strange place. More than a hundred tents were pitched in this international climbers' camp on the rubble-heaped moraines of the Khumbu Glacier. Sherpas from Namche Bazaar hiked up and sold Coca-Cola for seven dollars a bottle. People walked around, visited each other, shared stories, partied, and planned adventures. In general, it was a peaceful, idyllic spot.

7

DURING ONE OF OUR FIRST days in camp, a Buddhist blessing ceremony was held for us. In this way, all expeditions paid reverence to the mountain gods. This was not just a tradition; it was a necessity, because if you did not have such a ceremony, the Sherpas would not climb. The blessing, or *puja,* is surrounded by superstition. An accident at the start of the season in the Icefall had already been connected with it. Three Sherpas from Mal Duff's expedition were establishing the route through the Icefall. One of them had not yet attended the blessing ceremony. They crossed a snow bridge over a crevasse, and the bridge supported the first two (who'd already been purified in their *puja*) — but the bridge collapsed under the weight of the third, unblessed Sherpa. He fell fifty feet and broke his thigh. The fact that he fell was a sign, the other Sherpas claimed. He had challenged Chomolungma.

Our ritual took place around our stupa, a stone monument with a ten-foot-high wooden pole sticking up from it. From the top of the pole, four strings stretched in each of the cardinal directions and were anchored to the ground. Hanging from the strings were multicolored Buddhist prayer flags. When each cotton flag flapped in the breeze, prayers were carried aloft to Chomolungma by a divine wind. I liked the thought.

An old, bald-headed lama pressed his knuckles together and rocked back and forth while reeling off prayers in a mysterious tongue. Then he grew quiet. A fire was lit. The dark smoke enveloped us, and we threw rice and flour at the stupa. Then we ate some nuts and a little Buddha statue of sugar and butter, and drank a spoonful of beer. I did it, too. I was eating things I had not brought with me from home—a small sin, committed in the name of the mountain god.

Ang Rita, of course, was present at the ceremony, and he watched us meekly with his furrowed, reddish-brown face and dark eyes. He was a squat little man, and his tan was the darkest I'd ever seen. His skin looked like leather.

"Many people wonder, 'What is Ang Rita like?' They imagine me as a big, strong, successful person," he told Wendy Brewer Lama in an interview. "But when they meet me, they see I am just a simple man. I wear a T-shirt, I live in an old stone house, and I never went to school."

Still, Ang Rita had received almost all of the honors Nepal could offer. He'd made money, too, but to tell the truth, he'd wasted some of it on booze. He often reeled around in Namche Bazaar like a drunk war hero, but the Sherpas probably thought, well, he deserves his drink. In the Khumbu Valley, Ang Rita Sherpa was king. He was born not far from here, by the old trade route to Tibet. His family grew potatoes, but since the farming couldn't support the family, he started working as a porter for mountaineering expeditions.

"Since I had no education, I could find no other work; there aren't many paying jobs in the mountains. . . . I knew that climbing was dangerous, but I had no choice. People said that some day I wouldn't come back."

On May 7, 1983, he scaled Mount Everest for the first time, climbing with an American expedition. On October 15, 1984, he summitted again, in horrible weather, working for a Czechoslovakian team. The Czechs had hardly any money to pay him, and he made the ascent dressed in a worn-out down jacket minus the feathers. It's a miracle he survived. By 1996, Ang Rita had scaled Mount Everest nine times — far more times than anybody else, and he'd always done it without using bottled oxygen. His is an unparalleled achievement — and he's fifty-seven years old, not a young age for a climber.

"But what am I to do?" he has said. "Everybody tells me to stop, but I have four kids to support, and I want them to have a chance to go to school. I will keep climbing as long as I can. Perhaps I'll die up there and be buried in heaven."

I heard about Ang Rita early on, and I contacted him some time ago and asked if he could help me. I didn't need a Sherpa myself, but my filmmaker Fredrik did, and I also thought that it would be good PR to have the old legend on our team. Ang Rita accepted. He charged thirty dollars a day, which is a lot for a Sirdar — a head Sherpa — but Ang Rita stands in a class by himself in the Khumbu Valley. Now, he helped us bless our climbing gear. He told us to throw rice on our equipment and we took the ritual very seriously. We received small white scarves, which were supposed to bring us luck on the mountain. I glanced toward the Icefall. Its maze of ice towers and crevasses can be seen quite clearly from Base.

"Tomorrow," I thought to myself, "I will walk into that madness."

It was April 15, and I'd decided to climb through the Icefall without using any of the ladders and ropes other people have installed. I would make this part on my own, too. Somewhere inside me, I wondered if it was not an unnecessary risk. I had let myself be provoked by a blond, Swedish tabloid reporter. But mostly, I felt good about my decision. I was charged up. After the ceremony, I walked up to Ang Rita and thanked him.

"And now, hard work!" he said, in his usual abrupt way.

"What's the Icefall like this year?" I asked him.

"Troubled!" he said, smiling, as if he were talking about a human being.

I nodded and walked away. The sun was shining brightly. During the days, it was often warm in Base Camp. I saw a little bird on a rock, the only wild animal I'd seen up here. We were at an altitude of 17,100 feet, and climbers were just about the only creatures who lived at this altitude out of their own volition. Even goats and snow leopards rarely venture much above 16,500 feet.

Everywhere in camp, I met people I knew, and those I didn't know had heard all about my project. Veikka Gustafsson from Finland was here—he'd scaled more 8,000-meter peaks than any other Scandinavian. Lene Gammelgaard was here, too, the beautiful Danish woman who hoped to become the first Scandinavian woman to scale Mount Everest, and Mal Duff, the old Scotsman who came close to dying on Mount Everest in 1985. Duff was walking around Base Camp, asking $2,200 from each expedition for the use of the route that he and his Sherpas had just built through the Icefall. Many people got annoyed at this. But later, I learned that since 1988 it has been accepted practice for those who build the route through the Icefall to charge the others for it.

Back then, Rob Hall said that this was contrary to the ideals of mountaineering. However, he soon changed his mind, and when he helped prepare the route through the Icefall a few years later, he didn't mind charging the other expeditions. Which was more proof that Mount Everest was not just a mountain any longer; it was a business, too.

"I won't be using the normal route," I told Mal, when he stopped by. He looked at me in astonishment. But I paid him anyway, because Fredrik would follow the standard route. I was the only one who would use my own separate route through the Icefall. Many people had by now warned me against it, and I understood their concern. It was a dangerous variation I had in mind.

The Icefall is Everest's notorious trouble spot. From Base Camp, you could see how huge this wild mass of ice really was, plus you could hear it. The ice cracked, often like a gunshot, when it splintered. And it creaked and roared when new crevasses opened up, when towers of ice toppled over, and when avalanches rushed down through it. It was like a disaster area — or like a living organism. Dangerous, unpredictable, changeable, fickle.

When George Mallory first saw the Khumbu Icefall on July 19, 1921, he wrote that the glacier was "terribly steep and broken." He believed that it would be impossible to pass through it. He was wrong. Ninety percent of all Everest climbers today pass through the Icefall on their way to the summit, but the glacier gives a memorable fright to all. Eighteen people had ended their days here. I'd studied the Icefall carefully, and I didn't think that my route was more dangerous than any other. But it was a new route.

While walking around camp thinking about the Icefall, I bumped into Rob Hall. Rob wore a white cap and sported a thick black beard. He was urbane and relaxed, as became an authority like him. I could tell that he was in excellent shape. We wished each other good luck, and he thanked me, because he had bought into my climbing permit. Seven people are allowed to climb on one permit, which costs $50,000 for Mount Everest, so I had sold my spare places for $10,000 each, including spaces to three people from Rob Hall's expedition, among them Lou Kasischke, an attorney from Michigan, and Doug Hansen, a postal worker from Washington. Doug was one of the few American clients who didn't have a well-paid, high-status job. He had been working nights and had borrowed money to get here. Two Spaniards, the brothers Jesus and José Antonio, also bought into my permit.

Rob Hall's expedition tents constituted the nerve center of Base Camp. They had satellite dishes, a large stock of wine, a sound system, a small library, solar-powered lights, all sorts of telephones, and a large mess tent. But above all, it was Rob himself who gave the expedition status. He'd scaled Everest four times, more times than any other Westerner.

Rob was born in 1961 in Christchurch, New Zealand, the youngest of nine children. He hailed from the same country as Edmund Hillary and was friends with Sir Edmund's son, Peter Hillary.

The Hall family was Catholic and relatively poor. Rob dropped out of school at age fourteen, even though he was doing well and had a scientific mind. But he didn't just go climbing in his youth; he also designed and manufactured backpacks, tents, and mountaineering clothing. While still a teenager, he was hired by the company Alp Sports as a designer. When his organizational skills were discovered, he was promoted to production manager.

At age nineteen, he came to Nepal for the first time and scaled the beautiful peak Ama Dablam (22,402 feet). During the next few years, he continued to work for Alp Sports, but he also began working as a mountaineering guide, even leading scientific expeditions to Antarctica. On several occasions he climbed with his fellow countrymen Gary Ball and Peter Hillary. On May 10, 1990 — a date Rob would always remember — the trio stood at the summit of Mount Everest for the first time. While on top, they talked on a live broadcast on New Zealand radio and at 29,028 feet received congratulations from Prime Minister Geoffrey Palmer. Peter Hillary also spoke with his father over a satellite telephone.

That same year, Rob and Gary succeeded in conquering the Seven Summits — the tallest peak on each of the seven continents — in a seven-month period, a remarkable feat that was concluded at the summit of the Vinson Massif in Antarctica on

December 12, 1990. Rob was awarded the New Zealand medal that year. The year prior, he'd received an important honor from the Himalayan Rescue Association. Rob and Gary founded their travel and mountaineering company, Adventure Consultants, on the principle of anti-elitism.

"The mountains belong to everybody" was their company (and personal) philosophy, and Rob still claimed that he could get any decently fit person to the top of Everest. His statistics were impressive. In their brochure, Hall and Ball wrote:

> *Skilled in the practicalities of developing dreams into reality, we work with you to reach your goal. We will not drag you up a mountain—you will have to work hard—but we guarantee to maximize the safety and success of your adventure.*

In 1992, they ushered six clients to the top of Everest, and the next year seven. But that was also the year when Edmund Hillary first criticized them and talked about the sad commercialization of Mount Everest. Hillary is as important a national figure to New Zealand as our king is to Sweden. To be criticized by him, particularly if you are a climber, hurts bad. In October 1993, Rob Hall also lost Gary Ball, his closest friend and business partner. In a way, the drama started a year earlier when the pair climbed K2. High on the peak, Gary suffered severe pulmonary edema. He was unable to move. A hard gale was roaring across the mountain, and while Rob desperately fought to save his partner's life, Scott Fischer—of all people—passed by their camp on his way down from K2's summit. He was accompanied by Charley Mace and Ed Viesturs (who was now one of the stars of the IMAX film team). With their joint efforts, they got Gary down and saved his life.

This was a clear indication that something in Gary Ball's physiology was no longer coping well with high altitude. But the very next year, Gary and Rob scaled Dhaulagiri (26,795 feet), the world's sixth tallest peak. Suddenly Gary collapsed. Soon after, he died from cerebral edema in Rob Hall's arms.

Rob did what many other climbers—me included—have done in that hurtful situation. He kept climbing, and he kept guiding on Mount Everest. The most renowned and experienced Everest guide ever, he asked big money. And even though other guides charged only a third of Rob's price, he was the most popular one.

But 1995 had not been a good year for him. Not far from the summit of Mount Everest, circumstances had forced him to turn his entire group around, even though the weather was fine and the clients begged him to go on. It was too late, Rob insisted. If they continued, they wouldn't be able to get down before dark, and then they'd be stuck on the mountain. He told them to descend.

It was a wise decision, but it put pressure on him. It wasn't easy to say no to clients who'd invested over $65,000 to make their dreams come true—even if you're Rob Hall. Perhaps that was the reason that he'd persuaded the postal worker Doug Hansen, who was with him that year, to return this season for a second shot.

This year, Rob promised Doug, he'd get him to the top.

8

I AROSE AT 4:30 A.M. THE night had been warmer than usual. I sat in my tent and filled my thermos with hot chocolate, then packed some crackers and dextrose in my backpack. It was time — not for the summit assault; no, not yet. First, I had to get acclimatized and set up my campsites, and the monsoon had to push the jet stream away from the mountain. But it was time to make a route through the Icefall.

Base Camp was asleep. The only sounds to be heard were cracks coming from the glacier and the rustle of the wind between the tents. I met up with the Spaniards Jesus and José Antonio, and we walked to the Icefall together. Once there, we went separate ways. The Spaniards took the standard route, while I walked to the left, following my own route, which no one had ever climbed before.

"I'll show her," I thought. "I'll show her damned tabloid."

It might seem petty to think about a Swedish tabloid at a moment like that, but a year ago, the same newspaper, *Expressen*, had attacked me. WARNING AGAINST KROPP'S HANG-GLIDING COURSE, read the headline, and in the article they claimed, incorrectly, that my course was of inferior quality and outright dangerous. The *Expressen* reporter who'd questioned the ethics of my Everest expedition just as I set out on my bicycle from Stockholm had suggested that my whole project would be hollow if I made use of the ladders and ropes that others had installed in the Icefall. While bicycling through Europe and Asia, I'd had plenty of time to think about this, and I decided I wanted to prove that I could make it completely on my own up Everest—even up the treacherous Khumbu Icefall.

The first stretch, up a ravine studded with white towers and boulders of snow, looked dangerous. I kept up a fast pace over the rugged terrain until I reached a rock outcrop that gave me some protection. I pressed myself up against it, panting, then I quickly untied my ice axes from my backpack. I solo-climbed up a vertical wall, then reached a place covered with stones and shattered blocks of ice. It looked like a battlefield where snowmen had had it out with each other.

It was still early morning. In the middle of the day, when the sun is hot, huge blocks of ice can break loose, and sometimes avalanches are triggered by the temperature change. The hours around daybreak are safer for climbing—safer, but not safe. The glacier is moving downhill all the time, its confusing and icy landscape changes continuously, and you never pass through the same Icefall twice. Towers of ice can come toppling down in the early morning, too, and snow bridges can break at any time of day. I climbed cautiously up some rocks, jumped between several blocks of ice, and walked over a fragile bridge of snow. In the distance, I could now see a caravan of people beginning their own struggles up through the Icefall.

It is a strange pastime that we share!

Fredrik was not far away, filming me through a telephoto lens. As always, Ang Rita was at his side. Then a third person appeared, a thin man whom I soon recognized as Rob Hall.

Fredrik said something to him, probably telling him what I was up to, because suddenly Rob shouted — but not without cordiality — "You crazy bastard!"

I suppose I might have been, but I did succeed in finding a new way through the Icefall. When I'd reached the upper section and finally stepped out in the Western Cwm, or the Valley of Silence as it's also called, it was as if I'd entered another world, a safe haven. The snowfield was solid and didn't slope much, and the view was beautiful and grand, both above and below. I sat down and drank my chocolate and was rather proud of myself. I was at 20,000 feet — approximately 3,000 vertical feet above Base Camp and not far from Camp One, or Advanced Base Camp, where many expeditions had already built up a fairly large staging camp.

"Göran, you old fighter. You made it!" I heard someone call.

"I've staked out the Kropp route!" I answered, with some attitude.

It was Fredrik yelling over at me. He'd made it up the standard route with the taciturn Ang Rita at his side. Even Ang Rita nodded as if to congratulate me. After a while, the two Spaniards appeared, and then a group of Danes that I'd met on Broad Peak. They all congratulated me — and admonished me. Everyone present was in perfect agreement that I really was a crazy bastard.

Then I took the standard route back to Base Camp. It had been a good day.

The strange life in Base Camp went on. The South Africans kept fighting with each other, and on the day that they threw out their physician, Charlotte Noble, she walked over to our mess tent. Charlotte was a tall, blond woman in her mid-thirties. Her voice was strained.

"Can I stay with you?" she asked.

"Sure," I said. "But I won't take responsibility for your climbing."

"I'm going to climb with Scott," she announced in a proud voice. "But . . . ," she added, hesitating.

"Yes?"

"Ian Woodall, our leader, is a jerk."

"So we've heard."

"He was given loads of money for the expedition, but we have hardly seen any equipment, so I need . . ."

"Yes?"

"A sleeping bag, some food, a tent, oxygen, and a permit to climb. Can you get me that?" she asked, sounding as if she were asking for a bottle opener.

"But you have a stove, at least," Renata said, mostly as a joke.

"Oh, yes . . . I guess I need a stove, too," Charlotte answered.

"I can get you a backpack," I replied, dumbfounded. "But the rest you have to get in Namche Bazaar. And remember, you must not climb until you have a permit."

Charlotte claimed that she'd climbed several mountains in the Himalaya, but strangely enough, she didn't even know how to put on her gaiters. As a rule, she refuses to listen to a word of what anyone tells her. The very next day she was out climbing without a shadow of a permit, and that was madness. She put my whole expedition at risk. If it got out that someone who claimed to belong to my expedition was climbing without a permit, the Nepalese government could send us all home—Renata, Fredrik, Magnus, myself, and all the others on our team.

"Take your stuff and leave our camp," I told Charlotte in a curt voice the next time I saw her. I had no choice.

Scott Fischer agreed. "I can't take responsibility for her either," he said. "There are too many amateurs on the mountain this year, and that worries me," he added, yet he didn't look worried at all. Scott never did. He was always wearing sunglasses and sneakers, and when I was around him, I felt like I was in a movie. He had charisma, and there was just something very natural about him that calmed you down. Still, I thought to myself, he must be under a lot of pressure, and later on it became evident that his relaxed attitude was partly a facade. Somewhere inside, Scott was tense, too.

His mission was to prove that he was worth the same high guiding fees that Rob charged, and a failure this year would be a big setback for each of them. But Scott had the media darling Sandy Pittman on his team, so that also put extra pressure on. It had also been rumored that Scott's health was not optimum, that he wasn't well, but I didn't know anything about that yet.

People often said that Scott Fischer was a survivor. Twice, he'd survived sixty-foot falls. As opposed to Rob, who carefully planned everything, Scott improvised and encouraged his clients to take some initiative. He was the artist of the trade, and the name of his company, Mountain Madness, was as significant to Scott as the name Adventure Consultants was to Rob.

"The main reason I guide is so I can go on my own adventures," he once told me. "We ought to go climbing together, you and me."

"Definitely," I answered.

"I want to do something cool on Kangchenjunga. We could bring one friend each. Wouldn't that be cool?" We also agreed to organize lecture tours for each other. Scott and I really hit it off.

Sometimes in the mornings, we'd see his glamour client Sandy posing in her various elegant outfits. She got up early to work with her press contacts and write her NBC Interactive Media journal. Now and then Sherpa porters came running to her carrying all sorts of important goods—for instance, *Vogue, Vanity Fair, People,* and *Allure.*

Sandy Pittman had already tried to climb Mount Everest twice, in 1993 and 1994. Chesebrough-Ponds sponsored her with $200,000 in 1994. In their ads, they called her a "world-class climber," which was a joke, considering that Sandy could get neither up nor down Everest without being ushered by her guides, climbers of the caliber of Scott Fischer. But you had to hand it to her, the lady was good at PR.

In interviews she referred to her climbing team in a way that made it sound as if she were leading the expedition herself, rather than paying big money for others to take care of her.

When a storm thwarted her plans to scale Everest in 1994, she got so mad that she tore the jewel-adorned gold cross from her neck—it came from Kieselstein-Cord, says *Vanity Fair*—and threw it into the wilderness. The Sherpas got upset. They probably thought it could have found better use to fund a school.

In 1993, she also climbed the Vinson Massif in Antarctica. The physician Beck Weathers, who was on Rob's expedition this year, was in Antarctica at the same time. Krakauer reported him saying that Pittman had brought a portable television, a video player, and "this humongous duffel bag full of gourmet food that took about four people to even lift it."

This year, Sandy seemed to have something going on with David Breashears, the filmmaker in the IMAX team who was her guide on Everest in 1994. At first, Breashears saw a lot of a certain Spanish woman, but now Breashears and Pittman were seen together—excuse me for gossiping—whispering to each other. One day we found out why.

Bob Pittman, Sandy's future ex-husband and cofounder of MTV, was involved in a new romance with the young designer Veronique Coa; up until very recently she had been married to David Breashears. So David and Sandy had been united by each having been jilted for the other's spouse. "They probably read invocations together," people said.

One day Sandy came to my tent to see me. Suddenly she was acting as if I existed. I wasn't just empty air any longer. I guess she'd heard about my project.

"I'm going to write a book," she told me. "I will call it *Summits of My Soul*."

"Nice."

"I want to interview you for the book, and I want to tell your story on my Everest Web site."

I nodded and answered politely, replying to Sandy's questions while she sat there with her little chic scarf and round sunglasses, interviewing me. She was swift and eloquent and had the kind of self-confidence that is bred in a person, I supposed, when you have millions of dollars. By now, all of Base Camp knew that she had become involved with a twenty-six-year-old snowboarder. It was the gossip of the day, and the Sherpas were getting increasingly worried. These love affairs—Sandy's with the snowboarder, Anatoli's with the woman who came to pay her respects to her dead husband, and others—make the mountain angry, they said.

The Sherpa Ngawang Topche was suffering from altitude sickness. When he didn't get better, even though he was brought down to lower altitudes, another Sherpa exclaimed: "Sagarmatha punishes us because people have had unclean sex on the mountain." These words became sort of a refrain that you heard every time the sky got dark. The mountain was God. Romances have brought bad luck. Here comes the storm.

But my thoughts were elsewhere. It was getting close to action now. I'd been studying the weather forecasts and had decided to start my ascent on May 1. On May 3, I hoped to be standing on the summit. There would be a full moon on these days, which would give me additional light in the early mornings. I'd been up on the mountain several times now to get acclimatized. On April 25, I slept in a crevasse at 23,900 feet. The walls were three feet apart, and I awoke to a frightening bang. I felt like I was in an elevator shaft and had heard the doors shutting high above. My blood went cold, and I waited for the block of ice that would kill me. But nothing fell. I still don't know what caused the bang. I crawled out of my sleeping bag and got dressed in the biting cold.

My fingers grew numb, and after a while, they started to ache. I was plagued by a desertlike thirst. It was a healthy acid test.

I'd also had many long talks with Fredrik Blomqvist and Magnus Roman. These were the guys I knew I could really depend on. Fredrik, who had hardly been up on a rooftop before coming here, was doing just fine at high altitude. We decided that he would join me up until 24,000 feet, filming with the Beta camcorder. Magnus was going to charter a single-engine plane, a Pilatus Porter. A wild ace pilot named Chrester was going to fly him over Mount Everest so that Magnus could take pictures of me at the summit. The difficult part was to coordinate everything. Renata would have a key role in this. The airplane had to set out at exactly the right moment.

Suddenly—while all this was buzzing in my head—I heard a terrible roar. I'd been writing a little in my journal outside of Mal Duff's tent, and talking with the Danish expedition. We were chatting about earlier climbs, but now we all jumped up.

"What was that?" someone cried out.

"An avalanche. It must be a huge one going through the Icefall."

"Is anybody there?"

"I'm afraid so. Scott Fischer and his team went up to reconnoiter."

"Damn!"

We dashed around, trying to get more information. A huge white cloud from the avalanche was rolling over the Icefall, the air blast hit camp next, then quickly the snow that had been thrown up into the air by the avalanche's impact fell over Base Camp. It was like a volcanic eruption. The air rumbled, and people ran all over the place, but no one knew anything, not yet. There was just a lot of hearsay. Finally a Sherpa came down and shouted: "Scott Fischer is safe! The avalanche missed him by an hour or so."

Scott, you old hero, I said to myself. You got away again.

Göran Kropp on Besseggen, Jotunheimen, Norway.   GERARD KROPP

Göran on Pik
Lenin in 1988.
MATS DAHLIN

Hang-gliding at Illampu in South America.

Mats Dahlin's ice axe with his picture and obituary on the top of Cho Oyu.

Mali, West Africa.

Göran in the district of Östergötland during one of the first stages
of the Everest expedition.

Göran at the fore-summit of Muztagh. K2 is seen in the background.
ANDERS RAFAEL JENSEN

Renata gives Göran a foot massage in Slovakia.

Göran in the Pakistan desert.

Göran on his
bicycle en route to
Kathmandu.
FREDRIK BLOMQVIST

Sleeping accommoda-
tions in Rumania:
together with rats in a
haystack.

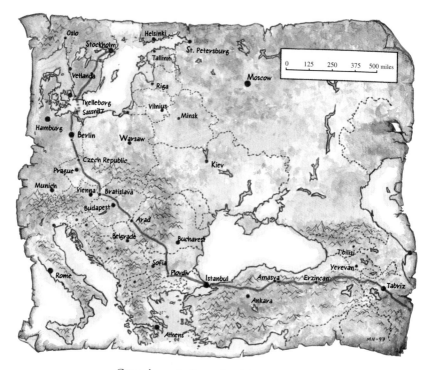

Göran's route from Stockholm to Nepal.

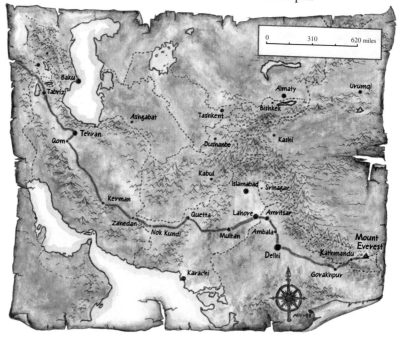

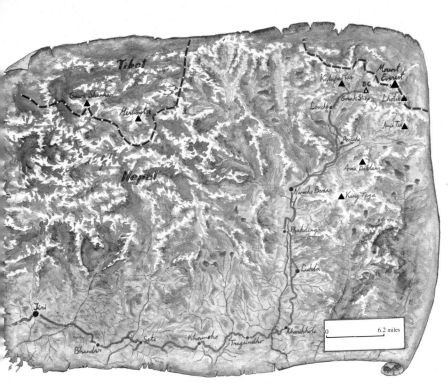

The approach to Mount Everest.

Göran during the approach.   MAGNUS ROMAN

MOUNT EVEREST

Göran's Route to the Top

▲ Base Camp 17,400 ft.
1. Camp One 20,000 ft.
2. Camp Two 21,300 ft.
3. Camp Three 25,400 ft.
4. Camp Four 26,200 ft.
5. South Col
6. South Summit 28,740 ft.
7. Hillary Step
8. Main Summit 29,028 ft.

Göran in Base Camp.
MAGNUS ROMAN

Göran on his way to Camp One.   FREDRIK BLOMQVIST

Base Camp at night.   FREDRIK BLOMQVIST

Göran on his route up Mount Everest.   FREDRIK BLOMQVIST

In Base Camp.   FREDRIK BLOMQVIST

Göran, standing at the South Summit, snaps pictures of people descending from the main summit.

Safe at last. Göran down in Base Camp after reaching the summit.

RENATA CHLUMSKA

Göran on the summit.   ANG RITA

Personal mementos at the summit of Mount Everest.

9

My ALARM CLOCK WENT off at 4:30 A.M. I hate to get up early, but this morning I woke without any problem. I was tense all over. Yesterday, I'd read a Stephen King novel and stuffed myself with the freeze-dried food I was so tired of eating. "Let me reach the summit the day after tomorrow, if for no other reason than because of the food. I want real food!" I thought to myself, but I immediately pushed that idea aside.

"Concentrate!" I hissed to myself. I got up and rechecked through my packing. Perhaps there was something I could take out. Your pack couldn't be too light up there.

I brought my stove, of course, and gas and food for six days. My rations for one day were two packages of crackers, four soups, one main course, and two army-issue chocolate bars, which are so hard that you could use them as weapons. I had my sleeping bag, ground pad, and one tent—I simply dismantled my Base Camp and packed it—two ice axes, one 165-foot rope, two ice screws, a headlamp, and a small camcorder.

Actually, I needed it all. Perhaps higher up I might leave some of the stuff behind, in a safe place so I could retrieve it later. We'd see. Then I dressed. I wore seven layers: underwear, a thin second layer, two thicker woolen layers, then something resembling a diving suit, a fleece sweater next, and finally my Haglöfs windbreaker.

No one had made a bid for the summit yet this year. I would be the first one. At 6:00 A.M. Base Camp was quiet. Someone coughed inside a tent, and a radio played almost inaudibly while I walked toward our stupa. I moved slowly, drowsy with sleep. I thought about the avalanche. I wondered if it had reshaped the Icefall, if it had affected my route. I would have to go and see. But first I had to walk three times around the stupa. It was a Buddhist custom observed by all climbers. When I reached the stupa, I saw that the prayer flags were almost still. They hung loosely, pointing toward the stony ground.

I walked slowly round the stupa. I thought about the summit. It was 750 vertical feet higher up than I'd ever been before, and I asked myself if those feet meant something from a physiological point of view. Would my heart and brain notice them? Then I set off for the glacier.

"Bye for a while," I said to no one.

The Icefall looked the same. I hurried through the bad parts of my route, but mostly it was all bad. I reached a snow bridge created by the wind. The fragile bridge spanned a crevasse. I inspected it. "It might support me," I thought. "Or perhaps not." I looked down in the crevasse and saw — or thought I saw — that it was only ten or fifteen feet deep, and that there was a bed of soft snow at the bottom.

"Pooh!" I mumbled. I took a chance and walked out on the snow bridge.

I heard a disquieting crackling sound. Something was happening under my feet. The snow bridge collapsed — and I fell down onto the soft snow — which was actually not the crevasse bottom at all but only a thin layer, masking a deep black well leading down into the underworld.

"Hell! Now I'll die!"

But somehow I stopped on top of the thin layer. The feathery snow held long enough for me to get out my ice axe, drive it into the crevasse wall, and anchor myself to it.

It was heavy work climbing back to the surface. I nearly did a full split bridging across the walls with my legs. I was exhausted. When my head popped over the rim, I saw a group of climbers in flashy clothes not too far away.

"Hey, I'm having problems!" I yelled to them—but they just waved back at me, unconcerned, and headed up the glacier.

"I can't believe it," I thought. "Damned $65,000 tourists. Idiots!"

I was furious. Strengthened by my anger, I hauled myself out of the crevasse. For a while I lay panting and out of breath on top of the snow. "Things like that could only happen here," I thought. "On any other mountain, they would have helped me." But Everest had become a luxury peak, a place for buffoons who wanted something to brag about at their garden parties. "A circus, that's what it is here."

It took me a while to calm down. Then I started off again. I got completely through the Icefall, kept going past Camp One, and headed straight for Camp Two. There's not much technical climbing on Everest. You mostly walk up endless slopes of snow, surrounded by giant, pyramid-shaped rocks. You feel small. According to the legends, Chomolungma gives life to the world through the rivers running from her glaciers. But Chomolungma doesn't just give life; she also takes it. The Sherpas believe she seeks revenge on people for their pride and lack of respect. Mount Everest can be furious, and sometimes, like today, I understand her fury.

After a while, I sat down to eat my lunch. Ahead of me was a giant snowfield, sloping only slightly, and suddenly I saw a character coming down from the mountain, walking slowly. It was a man in dark climbing pants and mirrored goggles. And wearing a baseball cap. Then I made out a ponytail. It was, of course, Scott.

"Hey, man!" he said.

"How's it going?" I asked.

"Good. It's cool. I've been up to the South Col. My team is ready for the summit now. We'll head up in a week or two."

"I'm going there now."

"Really? Good luck."

Scott sat down and searched through his backpack. He finally found a small, delicious-looking piece of cheese.

"Here you go," he said. "Eat it! It brings luck."

"Scott, you know my approach. I can only eat my own food."

"Oh, just eat it. I won't tell anybody." So I did as I was told, and while we sat there talking about what the summit looks like—because Scott had already been there—Fredrik and Ang Rita arrived. Fredrik was not feeling well; he was dehydrated. I got a bit worried that he hadn't been drinking enough—which was an easy mistake to make. In this dry climate, you not only lost two gallons of liquid a day, but the altitude also robbed you of any desire to eat or drink.

We rested for a while, said good-bye to Scott, then slowly, slowly walked up to Camp Two where we pitched our tent. It was 3:30 P.M. We were at 21,300 feet and before we prepared dinner we had several hours to kill. For some reason, Ang Rita suddenly became talkative.

"I've helped many people reach the summit," he said in broken English and, I noted, with a trace of bitterness. "I've done the hard part, carrying the loads up, and they have all become rich and famous. People climb the mountain with oxygen and guides and go back home and make lots of money. I climb without oxygen or anything, and I have to live in a stone house. What do you think about that?"

"But Ang Rita, you're famous, too," Fredrik said.

"Famous perhaps, but not rich. You know, the Indian government offered me to become an Indian citizen. They were going to give me a house and everything."

"Why didn't you move?"

"I didn't want to. My family is here. But I asked the Nepalese authorities if they couldn't offer me something instead. 'No,' they said. 'We don't give you anything.' "

Ang Rita turned down his dark face and looked at the snow. Now he was quiet, and after a while he went off to his Sherpa friends who had arrived. The rest of us melted snow and heated our soups. Which took a long time, an eternity. At high altitude, stoves have a harder time heating due to the lack of oxygen. At 26,000 feet, water boils at just 130 degrees Fahrenheit, which means that bacteria don't always die. And because of that, you can get sick even if you boil all of your water.

"How are you feeling?" Fredrik asked, while filming me.

I put up my thumb.

I could tell just what Fredrik was thinking: "Why does that bastard always have to put up his damned thumb whenever I'm filming him?"

I know the answer to that. I'm a cheerful devil. I have to be.

The next day, I joined Jesus and José Antonio, who had also decided to make a bid for the summit. After Fredrik and Ang Rita turned around at 23,300 feet, the Spaniards and I pitched our camp on a ledge at 25,600 feet. It was the day before the summit. Jesus and José Antonio unfurled their sleeping bags in my tent, but we hardly spoke to each other. We all knew that we had to get up around midnight if we wanted to reach the summit and get back down before dark tomorrow afternoon.

I lay in my sleeping bag, looking at the tent roof.

"I will make it," I thought. "It's going to be sensational . . . and then I'll . . . I will . . . get a hotel room in Kathmandu and order . . . No, don't anticipate! Don't do like you did on K2."

My thoughts continued to drone away inside my head. My thinking was sluggish. It's hard to be an Einstein at 8,000 meters. . . . The wind howled outside. The nylon flapped. Jesus and José Antonio breathed irregularly, panting.

It can drive you crazy sleeping in such close confines up here. You can't help listening to others' breathing. The breaths are deep and wheezy, then sometimes they go quiet. "Come on!" you think. "Keep on breathing!" But nothing happens, so you bolt upright, convinced that your partner is dead—and then he draws a long, bottomless sigh that seems to suck all the air out of the tent in one huge gulp.

But tonight I fell asleep, slept surprisingly well, and I dreamed a crazy dream, which I couldn't remember upon waking. There was just a vague feeling of something strange lingering in the air, and I twisted around in my sleeping bag and thought about how icy cold it would be as soon as I got out of it. But I fought off every impulse to stay where I was—safe in my sleeping bag, inside the tent—as if that thought itself would be deadly.

"How'm I actually doing?" I asked myself.

"Good," I decided. "Okay—I'm on my way."

José Antonio was in pain. He looked at me; his face was troubled. The two furrows on his forehead were new, and I could tell that he had an infernal headache.

"I'm turning back," he said. "My lungs hurt, too. I'm going down."

Jesus and I nodded. We went through our hopelessly drawn-out morning routines. We dressed in the biting cold, fiddled with our stoves, cursed the water that refused to boil, ate, checked our equipment. This took two hours. Then we got out, shivering for a moment before making our way into what journalists love to call the Death Zone, the realm above 8,000 meters. The snow crunched under our feet. There was a wind, and I walked with my head bowed. I felt strong. Soon we reached Camp Four—the South Col, a.k.a. "the world's highest junkyard." When I saw the camp, I understood why. The South Col is a giant plateau, the size of a hundred football fields. There were already four abandoned tents here, each shaking furiously in the gusts, and all over the place were oxygen bottles, ropes, trash, and a couple of long, white and blue bags. I knew far too well what was inside them.

"Don't think about them," I told myself. "Just keep on moving."

I crossed the frozen plateau and reached a series of gullies leading toward the upper Southeast Ridge and Everest's South Summit. "What did Scott say?" I tried to remember. "Follow the right gully, then make your way up onto the main ridge as soon as you can." I panted heavily, and I had to stop often. No one had been here yet this year, so there were no tracks to walk in, and it was unbelievably hard work breaking a path through the deep snow. Jesus was exhausted, so it was up to me to break trail. At 27,200 feet, Jesus turned around. He headed back down.

"Am I too tired, also? No, no! But what time is it?" I wondered.

I didn't know, and at this altitude you have to know. To forget the time can be fatal. If you climb without oxygen, you must never get to the summit after 2:00 P.M. If you do, you won't make it down before dark. At 2:00 P.M., you must turn around, no matter how tantalizingly close to the top you are. I had my watch, an Avocet, with me, but it was under my jacket and all my other layers of clothing, and the cold was biting. I didn't dare roll up my sleeve to take a look at it; I was afraid I'd get frostbite.

So I called Fredrik and Ang Rita on my radio. I was breathing so deeply that I could hardly speak. I just wheezed.

"I'm close to the South Summit," I said. "What time is it? Should I continue?"

Ang Rita answered: "Just continue. Go on!"

The radio crackled. Ang Rita's voice was blurred. I didn't have the energy to talk anymore, and I wondered: "Did we understand each other correctly?" I got scared. To my left, I saw—as if I didn't understand the seriousness of the situation enough— another white body bag, and next to it, a few oxygen bottles. The view of the landscape far below was phenomenal, with cloud banks and 23,000-foot peaks. I could gaze out over the world: China, India, Nepal. I was so high that I could see the curvature of the horizon; I could see that the Earth is round. But to be honest, I was too tired to appreciate it, and furthermore, just then I heard the sound of an engine. It sounded like an airplane . . . like a Pilatus Porter.

"No, no!" I thought and got out my radio.

"What the hell!" I coughed. "I have an hour left to the summit. Why is the plane up now?"

"We don't know," Fredrik said. "It must be because of the weather. It's turning bad."

Meanwhile, Renata was waiting for us in Base Camp. She'd been sleeping on the floor of the tent next to the communication radio. She was tired and stressed and feeling helpless. But no one had died on the mountain this year, so she wasn't as afraid as she would later be. Mostly she worried that I would fail, not because it was that important to her personally, but because she knew what it would mean to me. That was her fear now, nothing worse than that, nothing fatalistic—or fatal. She hadn't seen the blue and white body bags up where I was. For now, she still saw mountaineering as a relatively safe activity.

Of course, she'd heard stories of people dying on the mountains, but the concept was, as yet, unreal and distant to her, especially now when people in Base Camp were partying and frolicking. Renata is not naive, but it wasn't long ago that she didn't know anything about mountaineering. Then she met me and was drawn into a new world—a classic life story for a woman, perhaps.

Still, Renata had taken command in Base Camp; she was in charge while I was climbing. The frustrating problem was that we couldn't communicate directly with each other. I was too high up. So in order to ask me something on the radio, she first had to contact Fredrik at Camp One, who was at 20,300 feet with Ang Rita, and then Fredrik would relay her questions to me.

A couple of days before, Renata had attended a party with Rob Hall's expedition. She sat beside the Japanese woman climber Yasuko Namba. This would give her an eerie feeling later on, but at the party, people were in high spirits. They ate and drank, and Rob's Base Camp manager Helen Wilton and some others danced on top of the table. It was a real party—the last one.

But Renata wasn't really in the mood for partying. She was glad to meet new people, and now that I was gone and headed for the summit, happily some of them dropped by our mess tent. (I also had an excellent ambassador in Renata, who always greeted everyone with her beautiful brown eyes.) Soon there was a crowd. All of Base Camp seemed interested in my climb. Helen Wilton even hung up a sign saying, "Go, Göran, Go!" on their mess tent. Perhaps it's natural for people to get so involved in someone else's project, especially if it's somewhat different than the norm.

"How is Göran doing?" Veikka Gustafsson, the Finn, asked Renata.

"Göran has left his backpack behind. He's going for the summit now," she told him.

"That's good," Veikka said. "That shows Göran is being rational."

"What do you mean by that?" she asked.

"Some people who climb without oxygen get confused up there. But Göran knows that he has to be as light as possible. He's thinking clearly."

At that moment, Rob Hall dropped by our tent, too. Renata thought he looked relaxed in his cap and his black, straggly beard. He walked up to her and extended his hand. "Stay cool," he said. "Your boyfriend is damn good. He's gonna be all right!"

This flattered and reassured her. "When Rob, the great mountaineer, says everything will be fine, then it will be," Renata thought to herself. If anyone at Base Camp knew what he was talking about, it was Rob. He projected knowledge and competence. Then Renata heard the airplane.

"What's this?" she exclaimed, seeing $5,000 go down the drain. "It's too early! Julle, Julle! What are you doing up there?"

Magnus Roman—Julle, as he's called—was up in the single-engine plane. He was warmly dressed, wore a harness over his clothes, and was now frantically trying to sort out what to do. He'd had a thousand questions he wanted and needed to ask Chrester, the pilot, before they'd taken off, but Chrester had treated him in a surprisingly nonchalant way when they'd met at the small Namche Bazaar airstrip. Perhaps Chrester felt he was entitled to his attitude. In Namche Bazaar, he was a big hero. Everybody knows Chrester is the only one who can make difficult precision flights between the peaks around here. But he's macho, too, and didn't even explain to Magnus how the oxygen equipment worked.

Chrester was piloting the Swiss-made Pilatus Porter, the only single-engine plane that can reach 29,500 feet, which is how high Magnus needed to be to take pictures of me at the summit. But when the two met at the airport, Chrester seemed to have forgotten about their deal.

"I won't fly above 20,000 feet," he said in a firm tone of voice, indicating that the topic was not open for discussion.

"Well, what am I doing here?" Magnus told him. "Then we've spent $5,000 on nothing."

It wasn't until they were up in the air and alone—flying alarmingly close to the mountain face of Ama Dablam—that Magnus realized Chrester's statement was for the benefit of the Sherpas in Namche Bazaar. Chrester didn't want anybody to know what he and Magnus were going to do, and to start with, single-engine planes are not allowed to fly higher than 20,000 feet.

The summit of Mount Everest may be as small as a snow-drift in a school yard, but it belongs to two separate countries: Nepal and Tibet (currently an autonomous region belonging to China). If your goal is to circle around the summit of Mount Everest in a plane, then you will inevitably violate Tibetan-Chinese air territory, so you'd better have a few pretty good excuses. Swedish newspapers later reported that our plane couldn't steer properly and experienced some serious rudder problems. I don't know; I wasn't there, but maybe it did.

Magnus and Chrester circled upward in the Pilatus Porter as if they were riding along an invisible mountain road. The cockpit was wide open. Even in this biting cold, Chrester wore only gabardine pants and ordinary shoes. The only thing missing to complete the comical picture of this Himalayan Red Baron was a long scarf blowing in the wind. But Chrester's face was obscured; he, too, breathed through an oxygen mask, taking in lungfuls of oxygen via a supply tube as thick as a vacuum-cleaner hose. Magnus, sitting in the rear seat, had to make do with a lousy little mask equipped with some flimsy tubing.

"Does this thing work at all?" he wondered nervously.

They had, more than likely, left the airport too early. The plane wasn't supposed to leave until they'd received a go-ahead radio call from Base Camp, which wouldn't be made until I was approaching the summit. But while they were waiting, in his typical, self-assured way, Chrester stated: "Let's go. It's now or never. The weather is turning bad." So Magnus already knew that the odds for getting the pictures of me on top were slim.

"I'll have to make the best of it," he thought. "Let's see . . . Where should I fasten myself in?" Magnus anchored a short length of rope from his harness to two separate places in the cockpit. Then he put on his oxygen mask and prayed that it would work better than it looked. Even world-class mountaineers can just barely breathe above 29,000 feet—and that's only after becoming fully acclimatized over a period of a month or two. If Magnus, who in the plane would obviously ascend rapidly to this elevation, didn't get a sufficient oxygen supply, he'd die.

To his right was a sliding door. Magnus opened it—and was struck by an ice-cold blast of wind which, including the wind-chill factor, might have been minus ninety degrees Fahrenheit. With his face protected by his woolen balaclava hat and oxygen mask, Magnus leaned out of the plane, and, yes, he almost felt that he could touch Mount Everest. Chrester, the madman, was flying frighteningly close.

Magnus had a High-8 camcorder plus a still camera. He started taking pictures while at the same time frantically looking for me. Suddenly, he experienced an intense feeling of panic, an exploding sensation of mortal dread. He clutched his throat; he couldn't breathe. He looked around the cockpit in desperation but didn't understand what was happening; he did realize that he had to check his equipment. Finally—he saw it.

His oxygen tube had come off the fitting! He was not breathing any fresh oxygen. He tore off his mask and his hat. He was so desperate that luckily he focused only on what he had to do—and not on the ice-cold wind now blasting against his unprotected face. After hooking up the oxygen tube, he put his mask and hat back on. It was a small miracle that Magnus was so methodical. Meanwhile, the plane had just reached the level of the summit. They were circling it. It was a grand and unbelievable sight. The lower surrounding peaks stuck up through the thin cloud cover far below them.

The wind and the cold made his eyes tear up, and often Magnus couldn't see what he was shooting pictures of. But then he saw something red, something red right at the summit, and it looked like a human being! He knew that I was the first climber this year to head for the top, so it must be me, he thought excitedly.

"Is it really true? Is he already there?" Magnus wondered.

I was standing in front of three small, steep peaks. I waved frantically to the airplane up above, but no one seemed to see me. The plane just kept circling, and after a while it descended into the valley and the sound from the engine died away. I looked around. I was standing on a narrow ridge, the dividing line between Nepal and Tibet. A 10,000-foot drop welcomed me on each side, but the sense of exposure didn't bother me. I ignored it. The strange thing was that I couldn't orient myself to exactly where I was on the mountain. "That must be the South Summit up there—only 150 feet higher," I thought. "Because it can't be . . . the main peak? The highest point in the world."

I got out my radio again and described to Fredrik in Camp Two what the landmarks around me looked like, then Fredrik relayed the information to Ang Rita. Apparently, the Sherpa used his hands for a map; his bony fingers became the rocks of Mount Everest. It was probably not the world's best map, and it kept changing as Ang Rita moved his fingers.

"Ang Rita says . . ." Fredrik hesitated. "He indicates . . . that you ought to be somewhere . . . close to those rocks that are like a thumb and an index finger . . . like a hand. . . ."

"Damn it, Fredrik! Tell him that there are lots of loose ropes here!"

"Many ropes?" I heard Ang Rita say.

"Yes!" I panted.

"Many ropes everywhere?" Ang Rita asked in reply, and for a moment I thought he sounded just like the waiter Manuel in the British TV comedy show *Fawlty Towers*.

I was about to go crazy not knowing where I was, but with

Ang Rita's help, many long minutes later I finally figured out that I was on top of Everest's South Summit at 28,700 feet.

Feeling increasingly nervous, I finally asked them what time it was.

"One-thirty," came the answer.

Those numbers were my verdict, and the decision I had to make was bad. "Damn it!" I thought. "I could have made it!" But the harsh truth was that I was still about an hour from the summit. I hadn't left my top camp until 2:00 A.M., which was too late, and now I didn't have enough time to reach the summit — and descend safely — before dark.

"Next time, I'll have to leave the South Col before midnight," I muttered and turned around. Even though I was only 350 vertical feet from my goal, I had to descend.

Even moving downhill, I began to notice how tired I was. I decided to sit in the snow and slide like a little kid on a slope in his backyard. It was scary; I got going too fast and almost lost control of my glissade. I had to use my ice axes to slow down, but I saved time and energy by sliding. Bad weather was coming. Mists slowly closed around me, and when at last I reached the South Col, the whole sky was clouded over. Soon, I couldn't see a thing. I stumbled, staggered, and mucked about. I could feel the storm approaching.

"Where's the camp? It's got to be here somewhere. It's got to . . ."

Then I stumbled over something. An oxygen bottle. I was in the middle of camp, surrounded by junk and body bags. For a moment, I considered spending the night here, but I staggered on, descending toward the tent the Spaniards and I had pitched a little farther down.

"Hola, señor!" Jesus shouted a little later.

I didn't answer him. I hadn't enough energy. My head felt as if the storm and clouds had entered my brain. I collapsed in the tent into something resembling a coma. I have only a faint memory of the Spaniards shaking me.

"We're going down. Right now. You, too! Storm," they said. "Are you coming?"

"No," I said. Or perhaps I muttered something inaudible to them. In my haze, I was not aware that my life was in danger. Somewhere, I knew that I couldn't stay up here any longer, but I had to rest . . . just rest a little. The hours passed. Now I was alone; the Spaniards had left. More than a full day went by, but of that I can remember only single, scattered moments. I had a faint idea that a night had passed, too, but how long ago was that? And what time was it now? For that matter, what day was it?

I lay still and concentrated. Then I got up, on my knees first, and stood, which required an absolutely superhuman effort. I looked outside the tent. "It can't be true," I thought. My blood grew cold. Outside, the sun was about to set. Another night was descending on the mountain. I rushed inside the tent and got ready in a hurry. "I have to get down!"

Back outside, I looked again at the sun. It was a strange color, so pale-looking, as if it was dying and the whole world was turning into a freezing-cold Everest.

"Damn it, Body!" I cursed myself, shaking my head in disbelief. "Don't be such an idiot! The disc up there is the moon, not the sun, and it's morning, not night."

Ang Rita and Fredrik sat snugly in Camp Two. The old legend and the blond, small-town Swede who usually worked for a local TV station had somehow found one another. During their lengthy wait, they had several long discussions about Mount Everest.

"Mountain, not rock. Mountain is God," Ang Rita said sometimes, when Fredrik made some irreverent comment about Everest.

At this time, neither of them knew that Magnus Roman thought he had taken pictures of me at the roof of the world. They also didn't know that the red dot on Julle's pictures was not me, but a measuring instrument left on the summit. But Fredrik and Ang Rita did know that I hadn't made the summit, because the two Spaniards had already been by on their way down to Base.

"But what's taking him so long?" Fredrik asked.

"Mountain is tough! Hard to walk," Ang Rita replied.

In their almost unintelligible English, the Spaniards had told Fredrik and Ang Rita: "Göran very tired," but they didn't say anything more to indicate that my exhaustion was of quite another dimension than the tiredness a runner experiences after a hard race. My exhaustion was such that it could not be remedied by sleep. My exhaustion felt deeper than a grave. Veikka Gustafsson, the Finn, was also at Camp Two; there they anxiously awaited my return.

"Do you see him?" Renata asked over the radio from Base Camp.

"Not yet, not yet," was the answer—again and again and again.

Uphill in front of Fredrik, Ang Rita, and Veikka rose an endless snowfield dotted with small round hillocks. And they could hear, coming from the direction of the summit, the continuous roar of the jet stream wind. A while later, Fredrik spotted something through his telephoto lens. It was a gangly man who stopped and rested every two steps.

"It can't be Göran," he thought. "Göran is not that skinny."

But then he recognized me. He flinched. I was bearded, my lips were dark, almost black, and my nose was burned and swollen. The worst thing was that my body had changed so dramatically. In the course of just a few days, the mountain had consumed my muscles. I was emaciated and gaunt. My legs wobbled beneath me.

"I've given all I have," I said when I reached them, and my eyes filled with tears. I wept openly and sat down in the snow and tried to tear off my crampons and boots. Then I fell asleep under the open sky. I didn't even bother to go inside the tent.

The next day, Renata paced back and forth in Base Camp. Before I fell asleep at Camp Two, I talked to her, or rather, I wheezed and panted over the radio, trying to talk to her, and that's when she realized how tired I was. But even though I barely had the strength to think, and everything just felt empty and hollow, I already knew that I wouldn't give up yet. I did realize, however, that now I would have to yield on some of my strict rules. To get enough energy to scale Mount Everest, I would have to eat something other than freeze-dried food.

But Renata was wondering if everything was all over now. If I was completely defeated. She felt awful. She didn't know whether she should encourage me to try again or just say: "Three-hundred and fifty vertical feet from the summit is a feat, too. Let's go home." She felt that whatever she said, it would be wrong. Today was May 6, 1996.

Rob Hall and Scott Fischer had also been pacing around Base Camp. And they had declared that the tenth of May was their summit day.

"We don't want any amateurs on the mountain that day," Rob proclaimed publicly. No wonder there was tension in Base Camp, because what if the tenth of May offered the best climbing weather of the season? Many other climbers were now openly annoyed by Scott and Rob's demand for exclusive rights to the summit that day.

"No one gives me orders," the South African leader Ian Woodall raged, to no one's surprise. "We ascend whenever we want to! If anyone has a problem with that, I'll personally make sure they go to hell!"

Rob Hall, I knew, had several reasons to choose this day. Two of his four triumphs on Everest had taken place on May 10. But Rob—the guy with an analytical mind—was not concerned just with lucky numbers. The days around the tenth day in the fifth month of the year have always been considered ideal for climbing the mountain, and the number of people who have reached the summit around that day is astounding. On this day, there is often a window, a pause between the two rulers of the stratosphere: the jet stream and the monsoon. But this window might open only briefly, like a moment of stillness, a minute of silence, between the two competing storms.

Monsoon clouds are formed when water vapor from the Indian Ocean and the Bay of Bengal condenses in the atmosphere. Then the air currents blow the monsoon toward Everest—and if the circumstances are right, they in turn push away the jet stream winds which have raged over the mountain all winter and spring. That is the moment of calm climbers seek, coming after the winds have abated a little, but before the monsoon arrives in full force and envelopes the mountain in a shroud of storms and torrential rains.

The mountaineers in Base Camp were waiting for the sky to grow quiet, for one or two days—so Rob and Scott's demand caused considerable annoyance.

I was the only one who didn't care. I was exhausted, and while other climbers were discussing winds and climbing schedules and arrogant mountain guides, I came walking out of the Icefall looking like a wreck.

"Sometimes you're so tired you don't care if you live or die," I had said earlier into Fredrik's camera. Now I staggered into Base. My helmet was red, my pants were black, and my face was approaching green. When Renata met me outside her tent, I was walking unsteadily. My eyes filled with tears, and for some reason I stared straight up, as if I were looking for a star in the sky in the middle of the day.

"I've given all I have," I said again, and I almost fell over backward. Renata also cried; Jesus helped me take off my backpack.

Later, when I saw this meeting replayed on video, I could barely grasp that this gaunt man, showing all the whites of his eyes, was me. In retrospect, it is not hard to understand Renata's shock when she saw me like that. No one could talk to me, I was so completely done in. And Renata didn't know if she should comfort me or try to pep me up. I was too tired to be able to give her any clues. Renata had fallen in love with a Göran Kropp who was happy and optimistic. Now she sat crying in front of someone she did not know.

10

THE FIRST THING I DID IN Base Camp was to devour an entire can of butter. My body was crying out for fat. I built little mountains of butter on crackers, and ate them in a feeding frenzy. Then I collapsed and slept. All the while, Renata lived on tenterhooks, wondering, "What is he thinking? Is he really going to try again? Is that even possible?"

On top of this dilemma, the rest of Base Camp's many occupants were getting ready for their summit attempts. I could tell that everybody around me was charged — everybody but me. I was totally knocked out. I didn't even want to wake up.

The Texas physician Beck Weathers, who would soon celebrate his fiftieth birthday, had recently called his wife, Margaret, nicknamed Peach, in Dallas. He told her everything was fine. Weathers had met Rob Hall in Indonesia a couple of years before and was so impressed by Hall's record as a guide — Hall had by then ushered thirty-nine people to Everest's summit — that Weathers paid his $65,000 to be on this year's trip. This was not a paltry sum, not even for Weathers, a well-off pathologist. Weathers's political views were to the right of Reagan's. Sometimes he called himself, jokingly, "a health nut and a training freak," and for several years now, he'd been climbing one big mountain or so a year—but none as tall as Everest, none that had even come close.

"I've always been afraid of heights," he told me. "But when I turned forty, I thought it would be interesting to defy my fear and see what would happen."

Beck Weathers, the son of a U.S. Air Force officer, spent his childhood on military bases. After college, he studied medicine, married Peach, and had two children, Beck II, now seventeen, and Mag, fourteen. As a successful physician, he played golf and tennis, but it wasn't until 1986, when he vacationed in Colorado, that he began longing for mountains. Soon he told his wife that he, too— like fellow Texan Dick Bass, the inventor of the Seven Summits Club—was going to climb them all. This worried Peach, who sensibly realized that mountaineering was not the same thing as golf, even if both activities had become status sports for the rich.

Now, Beck Weathers had scaled six of the world's seven highest continental summits. Everest was the only one remaining, and when I woke up from my dreamless coma, Weathers and the others on Rob's team were ascending. Four expeditions were making their bids for the summit on May 10. Neither Ian Woodall and the South Africans nor the Taiwanese, led by Makalu Gau, gave a damn about Scott and Rob's directive to stay away that day.

One afternoon, Renata came into our tent with a strange smile on her face. I looked at her vacantly. I had by no means recovered yet.

"One of the Taiwanese is dead," she said. "He fell into a crevasse."

"That's nothing to laugh about," I told her, more curtly than I had to, and I quickly realized I should have spoken more gently.

For me, death on a mountain is a reality. It's something I was aware of even before Mats Dahlin died. The news of the death of the Taiwanese Chen Yu-Nan, a thirty-six-year-old steelworker from Taipei, was a painful reminder of something I already knew: Humans are very vulnerable up here. For Renata, life in Base Camp had been more like a pleasure trip so far. People ate peanuts and chips; they drank a little and talked loudly at parties. Chen Yu-Nan's death was unreal to her, and her smile expressed nothing but a kind of wonder and disbelief. It's the kind of face people show when they've heard something terrible has happened, but they don't yet know if it's true or not.

No one close to Renata had ever died, and I sensed what she felt when the Taiwanese climber was carried down in a blue body bag. Base Camp had lost its innocence.

On Thursday, May 9, the weather was perfect, as many had predicted. The South Africans seemed to have given up their attempt already, but Rob's team was in a good mood, at least considering the altitude. At 5:00 P.M., they reached Camp Four on the South Col at 26,200 feet. The last members of Scott Fischer's expedition arrived a little later. In their tents, the climbers tried to get some sleep. A sea of stars lit the sky, and the South Summit faded into a dark shadow.

In a few hours, they had to get up, ". . . but the machine-gun rattle of the flapping tents and anxiety over what was to come made sleep out of the question for most of us," wrote Jon Krakauer, who was on Rob's team. The postal worker Doug Hansen complained that he hadn't slept for days. Only two weeks before leaving for Nepal, he'd undergone throat surgery. Breathing the thin, dry air at high altitude, not surprisingly, hurt his larynx. Down at Base Camp I'd heard Doug say, time and again and with stunning bitterness, "I'm through. My adventure is over." But Rob Hall had done his utmost to encourage him, and it was clear that the New Zealand guide would do everything in his power to get Doug Hansen to the summit.

Doug was Rob's only team member who was not wealthy. And from my perspective, he might also have been the one who dreamed most passionately about scaling Everest. He told me he'd been thinking about it "every damned day—and every damned night" since a year earlier when Rob ordered him to turn around 350 vertical feet from the top. Doug was also one of the most experienced amateurs on Rob's team. He was divorced and still single— plus his kids, Angie and Jamie, had left home—so for the past fifteen years, he'd dedicated most of his energy to mountaineering. As opposed to a few other climbers on his team, Doug had some business being here.

Shortly before midnight, the climbers left the South Col for the summit. The comet Hyakutake could be seen in the sky, which worried the Sherpas. Many of the team were tired from climbing up to the Col and the lack of sleep. Several were plagued by harsh coughs. Still, there was confidence and assurance in the air. The weather was near perfect for a summit assault. The wind was surprisingly weak, and a large moon hanging above the peaks added its light to the beams from the climbers' headlamps. Initially, Beck Weathers took the lead, keeping up an impressive gait, but soon he slowed. Beck had recently undergone an operation to correct his eyesight, and when he got to Everest, he discovered that the lower air pressure at high altitude made it hard for him to see. Now, climbing above 26,000 feet, his vision was deteriorating. And, unknown to any of the climbers, bad weather was on its way; the atmospheric pressure was falling even lower.

Beck Weathers's eyes were sensitive to the change that was coming. Rob Hall climbed close to him, worried like a father. Somewhere below the South Summit, shortly after sunup, Beck admitted to Rob that he could hardly see. Rob decided he would have to go down, but Beck stated that he thought his vision would improve once the sun got higher in the sky. Rob reconsidered and told him to wait thirty minutes, and if his vision wasn't better by then, he'd have to wait where he was until Rob came back down and could help him descend to the South Col and Camp Four.

Rob continued climbing. His team had gotten delayed, and several of his clients were experiencing problems. Frank Fischbeck, a publisher from Hong Kong, had already turned back. Even Doug Hansen seemed about to give up, in spite of his dreams of the summit. For a while, he just stood immobile in the snow, looking like all of his strength had deserted him. Rob, the omnipresent guide, approached Doug and said something to him that no one else heard. The postal worker started climbing again. While the New Zealander supported the stragglers, his stronger clients waited for him higher on the mountain—because Rob's orders had been strict.

The team must not get spread out! But as a result of this order from Rob, both the Taiwanese climbers and Scott Fischer's team had all passed Rob. And knowing Rob, he felt pressured by this.

Scott, too, was working hard to support his team members, but he today appeared to be running low on his well-known physical strength. It was unclear what was happening. Perhaps he had exhausted himself during the last few weeks; he'd been up on the mountain constantly, instructing his clients, and preparing for the summit assault. "He'd been up and down that mountain like a German shepherd," Karen Dickinson later said.

Scott Fischer had stoic ideals. He would never openly complain, but he was suffering from an ailment that he'd kept secret. In 1984, when he had scaled Annapurna in Nepal, he'd suffered from a strange disease that affected his liver. During all the years since, he'd had several malaria-like bouts. And although he'd seen several doctors, none had been able to cure him. According to the journalist Jean Bromet, who wrote about the Mountain Madness expedition for *Outside* magazine's Web site, Scott had recently suffered several bouts, sometimes one every day.

Scott's best Sherpa, Lobsang Jangbu, was also tired. Yesterday he'd carried Sandy Pittman's heavy satellite telephone up to

Camp Four at 26,200 feet, and now, at dawn, to the surprise of the other climbers, he tied a rope to Sandy's harness and started dragging her up the mountain. The incident would later cause embarrassment in the New York press. Sandy would claim that she didn't want to be dragged like a plow behind an ox, that Lobsang dragged her against her will, and that it lasted for an hour and a half at the most. Others claimed the scene lasted six hours.

But Lobsang Jangbu, who loved and adored Scott like a father, knew how important Sandy Pittman was to the American mountain guide—she brought publicity and money—so when Lobsang saw the socialite lagging, he decided to do whatever it took to help her reach the summit. Lobsang was one strong Sherpa. But what he did—believe me—no one can do for long. Still, his assisting Ms. Pittman would play a crucial role in the drama to come, long after the two eventually untied from their rope.

The clock was ticking. Time began to run low. Some of the climbers thought it was too crowded on the mountain, but with everyone following the traditional Hillary-Tenzing route above the South Col, bottlenecks were bound to happen. When climbers ascend a length of fixed rope, only one or two can move safely on a single rope at a time—so those below have no choice but to wait. Plus the inexperienced Taiwanese were moving like snails and slowing down the pace for everybody, and Rob's failure to get any of his clients to the summit last year rested like an invisible weight on the shoulders of the guides.

Since no one had been to the summit this year either, no fixed ropes had yet been anchored for safety along the climb's final difficult passages: notably from the South Summit across to the forty-foot Hillary Step, then up it. The original plan had been for the Sherpas Ang Dorje from Rob's team and Lobsang from Scott's to climb ahead and fix the necessary ropes, but as we know, Lobsang had other things to do, and Ang Dorje thought he'd done enough already.

It was approaching noon. A group of climbers sat not far below the Hillary Step, the last vertical wall before the summit. Some of them had waited there for an hour and a half. All of them wore oxygen masks; it was hard to tell one from the other. The wind was howling. Jon Krakauer was one of the climbers; he felt groggy, as if nothing was real. Then he heard Neal Beidleman, one of Scott's assistant guides, say to Ang Dorje:

"Hey, Ang Dorje, are you going to fix the ropes or what?"

Ang Dorje still didn't see his colleague Lobsang. He looked disheartened, and his answer came like a whiplash: "No!"

Beidleman was perplexed, but he made a fast and good decision. Together with others in their cluster, Jon Krakauer and Mike Groom from Hall's team, and the Russian guide Anatoli Boukreev from Scott's, Beidleman started installing the fixed ropes himself.

Down in Base Camp, people were becoming increasingly worried. "Why hasn't anyone summitted yet?" was the eternal question.

"This too late, too late," the voice of experience, Ang Rita, muttered.

As the only climber left in Base Camp, I had plenty of reasons for being depressed. Everyone else was up on the mountain, and it made me sad to think that soon all of them but me would have reached the summit. But in the afternoon, my depressed feelings vanished, and my worry for Scott and the others took over. When it was well past 2:00 P.M., no one had yet—as far as we knew—summitted. We listened to the radio for news, and expected Rob Hall to give the turn-around order soon. We all knew how strict he was about timing, and I remembered how he'd praised me when I turned back at the South Summit a week earlier.

"That showed incredibly good judgment on Göran's part," he told people in Base Camp.

"Any bloody idiot can get up this hill. The trick is to get back down alive," Krakauer heard him say.

But time continued to pass with no news. When we met Rob Hall's Base Camp manager, Helen Wilton, she was getting desperate. It wasn't long ago that she'd been dancing on a table.

Renata and I looked at each other, and I thought to myself for the first time: "This is all going to hell."

Meanwhile, most of the climbers were still struggling up Everest's upper Southeast Ridge. Rob Hall got to the summit at 2:10 P.M., and that was late. Still, he lingered on top, waiting there for Doug Hansen to show up. No doubt Rob was thinking about last year's drama when he'd asked Hansen to turn around shortly before the summit, and perhaps he couldn't bring himself to say the same thing at the same place two years in a row—even if he should have, because he was the most rational man in the business. But Doug had not only worked nights and done construction work during the days to earn the money for this expedition, he'd also gone into debt. As he waited, Rob was disappointed that so many of his clients—Australian Dr. John Taske, Fischbeck, Weathers, American Lou Kasischke, and Hutchison—had all turned around before reaching the top. His statistics were worsening.

"I only wish we could have gotten more clients to the top," he told Jon Krakauer, who was on his way back down.

The sky was still clear. But the afternoon was waning, and behind Pumori and Ama Dablam, dark clouds could now be seen. A storm was on its way. Jon shook hands with Rob and pretended that he was in a better mood than he really was, so as not to seem ungrateful to his guide. Actually, Krakauer was experiencing a rising panic. He'd been on Everest's summit, with one foot in Nepal and the other in Tibet, and standing there he understood, he later wrote, "on some dim, detached level that the sweep of earth beneath my feet was a spectacular sight." He'd been dreaming about this sublime moment for years, yet when he finally stood on top of Everest, he couldn't muster the energy to absorb and savor it.

This may have been because Jon Krakauer hadn't slept for fifty-seven hours, and in the past three days he'd eaten only some M&M's and a bowl of soup. Now, to make things worse, his bottle of oxygen ran out. He felt close to fainting. When he got close to the South Summit, he saw Andy Harris, Rob Hall's assistant guide, sorting through some oxygen bottles cached there. He yelled to Andy to bring him a fresh bottle.

"There's no oxygen here! These bottles are all empty," Harris shouted back.

But when Krakauer got to the South Summit, he discovered that at least six of the bottles were full. Harris refused to believe it. Nothing Jon said could make him see reality as it was.

First you go crazy, then you die. That's what usually happens up here.

Shortly before 3:00 P.M., the ascending climbers were lined up below the Hillary Step. "It was so many people — like a supermarket," the Taiwanese Makalu Gau later told *Newsweek*. It was indeed true that a lot of people were now in a place not meant for humans, and especially not at this time of the day. The storm beat Makalu Gau to the summit, and when he finally got there, he saw hardly anything but prayer flags and the snow under his feet. The view was covered by clouds.

Neal Beidleman reached the summit with a group of climbers, among them Sandy Pittman. They exchanged a few tired gestures of triumph at the summit, then, after taking pictures, headed down. None of them could later remember whether Sandy had had the energy to bury her necklace from Barry Kieselstein-Cord at the roof of the world. But everybody sensed that Sandy was exhausted. On their way down, the group met Scott Fischer, who was still doggedly climbing up. He raised his arm in a tired greeting.

The star guide looked somewhat bewildered, and Beidleman was surprised that Scott was continuing upward at such a late hour, which went against all reason. Had it been someone else, Beidleman would have been alarmed. "But he was Scott, and I wasn't too worried about him," Beidleman said to Outside Online. He thought Scott would soon catch up and help the remaining slowest clients back down.

Scott summitted at 3:30 P.M., ninety minutes past the latest time you should be at the summit. On top, he met Lobsang Jangbu, who had been waiting for him for a long time. Earlier in the day, Lobsang had vomited from exhaustion. He had regained some of his strength, and he was moved as he received his mentor Scott Fischer.

Lobsang was twenty-three but already an experienced mountaineer. He had scaled Mount Everest for the first time in 1993, and the year after, he climbed with Scott Fischer on the Sagarmatha Environmental Expedition. They didn't reach the summit together, but they did help bring tons of trash down off the mountain. It was the beginning of a sort of father-son relationship.

Life reported that Lobsang had given Scott one of his earrings on the summit of Broad Peak, and that Lobsang had let his hair grow long and wore it in a ponytail, also like Scott. Later, Lobsang would visit Scott's office in Seattle and give Fischer's children a stone from the top of Mount Everest. Many people said that Lobsang and Fischer were much alike, and this flattered Lobsang. They were both strong climbers with strong personalities, and popular with women. Lobsang hoped the American would make him famous.

Now he was once again standing on the roof of the world with his hero. It was a crowded place. Rob was sitting there, too, still waiting for Doug. Makalu Gau was also on the home stretch, on his way up with two Sherpas.

"We made it," Scott said on the radio, before confessing he was tired. Lobsang realized that there was something going on with Scott, something strange. He was complaining, which normally he would never do—especially not in front of Lobsang. Now Scott told Lobsang that he was ill—and that he needed medicine.

A little later, Jeannie Price, Scott's wife of fifteen years, received a phone call at her home in Seattle. The couple had had their rough times. It can't have been easy to live with a charmer like Scott who was always traveling. Still, they'd always been very close, and if anybody knew what this expedition meant to Scott, Jeannie Price did. It would give them a good income, Scott would be independent of the money she earned as a pilot, and that would mean a lot for his sense of well-being.

"They've all summitted, and they're all fine," Jeannie was told.

Through the years, she had received several calls like that, but this was the first time Scott had been guiding on Mount Everest. Jeannie Price dashed to their children, Andy and Katie Rose, and told them.

Scott's business partner, Karen Dickinson, opened a bottle of champagne in the Mountain Madness office. According to *Life*, she then watered his plants, since he always accused her of letting them die while he was away on expeditions. She didn't know that a storm had broken out on Everest.

Hurricane-force winds were blowing. It was minus forty degrees, and in the driving snow, visibility was close to zero. Sandy Pittman had collapsed at the South Summit. She lay on her face and screamed to Charlotte Fox to give her an injection of dexamethasone—a substance similar to cortisone—straight through her clothes. Neal Beidleman rushed up to Sandy and made sure she got a new oxygen bottle to replace her empty one. Still, Sandy just wanted to stay where she was, so Beidleman began to drag her down by her harness, while urging her to walk. Fortunately, after a little while, the injection kicked in, and Sandy staggered downward under her own power into the white madness.

Scott Fischer and Lobsang were also headed down now. But the guide had problems standing upright; his legs swayed beneath him. After each couple of steps, he sat down in the snow to rest. Soon, he couldn't move at all.

"Go down," he said to Lobsang. "I'll stay. I'm too sick."

"I can't leave you, Scott. You know that."

"Go down. It's an order."

"Never!"

They were at 28,500 feet, trapped in a storm, and no one needed to tell Lobsang what would happen to Scott if he was left alone. Lobsang was in relatively good shape, but the guide had quickly deteriorated into a shadow of the man whom Lobsang had loved for years.

In mountaineering, there are several unwritten rules. First is that if a fellow climber becomes injured or hurt, you should do absolutely anything to help that you possibly can. Second, you should never leave a sick or injured climber alone. And third, only in a life-or-death emergency should you save yourself. This is what Scott was now telling Lobsang, to think of his own life. But no, Lobsang didn't want to leave Scott, and while he was thinking about what to do, the guide made a sweeping motion with his hand.

"I'll jump down to Camp Two," Scott said.

"What?" Lobsang exclaimed.

"I'm going to jump. It's no problem."

The sky was rumbling, the snowstorm roared, and a thunderbolt hit not far away. There was a tremendous bang and a strong flash of lightning. Scott no longer wore his oxygen mask, and it looked as if the wind might blow him away—if he didn't decide to jump, as in his confusion he'd said he would. Lobsang tied a rope to the American, who outweighed him by at least sixty pounds, and started dragging him down as darkness descended upon the mountain. It was an impossible endeavor. Lobsang had dragged one person too many that day. He kept at it until he was about to pass out. Then he anchored Scott to a rock. He leaned over him and prepared to say good-bye. Scott mumbled a reply.

At that moment, two other Sherpas came down the mountain. They were dragging the Taiwanese climber Makalu Gau, who was exhausted and in just as poor a condition as Scott. After a short discussion, the Sherpas tied Gau and Scott to each other.

Lobsang stayed with them for a while, then hurried down in the darkness and storm to get help.

Neal Beidleman remembered how a week earlier he and Scott Fischer had looked up into the heavens and identified the North Star.

"Keep looking up!" he shouted to the people in his group, when the clouds opened for a moment and several stars became visible. He urged them to keep moving and to not fall asleep in the whipping snowstorm.

But the climbers needed landmarks to follow if they were to have any hope of finding Camp Four on the South Col's wide-open plateau. The whipping snow had become so blinding that sometimes they could hardly even tell up from down. Furthermore, they were almost out of liquid to drink, and their food was frozen and inedible. Beck Weathers and the Japanese Yasuko Namba had already collapsed, and now Charlotte Fox and Sandy Pittman did, too.

"We just rolled up and waited to die," Charlotte Fox later said to *Vanity Fair*.

Anatoli Boukreev, the tough-as-nails Russian and former national cross-country ski coach for Kazakhstan, was already back at Camp Four. He and Beidleman were Fischer's assistant guides. The relationship between Boukreev and Fischer had been a tense one, and during Scott's last phone call—to Karen Dickinson at their Seattle office—he'd said strong words about how disappointed he was with the Russian. Anatoli wasn't doing enough.

He'd bedded the mourning widow, then earned additional notoriety by climbing sections of the route up Everest in a pair of running shoes. But Boukreev was a world-class climber, and now that Scott Fischer was still high up on the mountain, Boukreev and Beidleman had to take over.

After Anatoli had summitted, true to style he dashed back to the South Col. At 5:00 P.M., while his clients were struggling down the peak in the storm, Anatoli was sipping tea. Later, many would be upset by this—but Anatoli claimed that he knew the storm would overtake the slow clients, so he had arranged with Scott that he would descend to the Col to fetch extra oxygen bottles and thermoses of hot tea and carry them back up. Now Anatoli left the safety of Camp Four—and showed his truly heroic side.

He had tried to get other people to join him on a rescue mission, but those who had reached the tents were too exhausted to even answer him. The Sherpas at camp also refused to help. So Anatoli went out into the storm by himself to search for anyone he could find.

The blowing snow was like an impenetrable fog. He couldn't see anything until he finally saw the light from a headlamp. Then he heard a scream and saw a number of bodies lying on the ice, and he recognized Tim Madsen from Scott Fischer's team. Tim stared back at him. Next to him lay Sandy Pittman and Charlotte Fox, both of them unconscious. Beck Weathers also seemed beyond hope. Yasuko Namba appeared dead.

"Who do I take first?" the Russian asked himself. "Not someone who looks like they could make it a little longer, but neither someone who will die no matter what!"

With help from Madsen, Anatoli hooked up the oxygen bottle he was carrying to Sandy Pittman's mask. He then dragged Charlotte Fox for an hour until they reached the haven of Camp Four at 26,200 feet. Once again, Anatoli attempted to find someone who would help him on his rescue. No one would, so he went back out alone into the storm a second time. Next he chose Pittman. The socialite was semiconscious, and Anatoli had to partly drag and partly carry her. Meanwhile his thoughts were about Scott, as he later told *Life:* "I know Scott is thinking, 'Anatoli will help me.' I know he is waiting for me. Scott is strong. He will survive this night. But he needs help. Oxygen. Something to drink."

When Anatoli arrived at Camp Four with Sandy, he was exhausted. He had no more energy, no more strength, and he fell into a deep sleep, still thinking of Scott.

When Anatoli Boukreev woke the next day, he was sure that Beck Weathers and Yasuko Namba were dead. He'd seen them lying next to Pittman, Madsen, and Fox, and after a quick check, he'd decided they were beyond help. When Neal Beidleman learned that Namba was dead, he broke down and cried. Beidleman would never forget how he had tried to bring Namba to safety that night. Later he told *Esquire* that people had been shouting for someone to save them, and he had tried to get Namba to stand up. She had grabbed his arm, but she got up only on her knees, and he didn't have the strength to pull her more than a couple of steps.

"She was so little," he later said to Krakauer. "I can still feel her fingers sliding across my biceps, and then letting go. I never even turned to look back."

Anatoli was determined to enter the Death Zone again. He was going to rescue Scott. It wasn't until 7:00 P.M. that he found the American guide high on the mountain. Scott was alone. Some Sherpas had been there a couple of hours earlier and had saved the Taiwanese Makalu Gau. Anatoli checked Scott for any signs of life. There were none. Scott was gone. The American had lost one glove and his jacket was unzipped as if, oddly, he had felt warm during the night. In his ear was the earring Lobsang had given him, and around his neck, an amulet containing herbs, earth from his backyard in Seattle, and locks of hair from his wife and two children. Scott's hands were in a strange position—as if he had just been about to do something, whisk away a snowflake perhaps, but had frozen in midmovement.

Anatoli covered Scott's face with a backpack, then retrieved his ice axe, pocketknife, and camera. Scott's pictures would later be immortalized in *Life*. Then Anatoli turned away as darkness and the wind returned. He said he found his way back to Camp Four by heading in the direction of some strange screams that he heard. Somewhere up ahead of Anatoli, someone was walking, and screaming, in pain.

11

E ARLY IN THE MORNING of May 11, we heard steps outside of our tent. We unzipped the door and saw our liaison officer — the Nepalese authority in charge of keeping an eye on us.

"We think twenty people are dead," he said.

"What?" I exclaimed.

"Don't say anything on your satellite phone. Nothing must come out yet."

Base Camp was in a state of total confusion. One rumor was replaced by another. Suddenly only ten people were missing, then the figure went up before going back down again. But soon it became all too clear that Rob Hall and his client Doug Hansen had been trapped in the storm close to the summit. Scott and Makalu Gau had disappeared, but there was also information that they were sitting high on the mountain, tied to each other. To me, that sounded incredible. What was Scott doing climbing with an amateur like Gau?

Yasuko Namba, whom Renata had gotten to know a little

bit, was apparently dead, as was Beck Weathers. Rob's assistant guide Andy Harris was missing, and three Indian climbers who had ascended the opposite side of Everest via the Northeast Ridge in Tibet, we also heard, were in mortal danger. Since there were almost no climbers left in Base Camp, I realized I had to do something.

"Can you climb up there with medicine?" I was asked.

Ang Rita and Kami Sherpa had also been asked to go up, but they had refused. They didn't want to challenge the mountain god.

"The mountain is angry," they said over and over. "People have not been acting with dignity."

It was around noon, the most dangerous time to be in the Icefall, so my modest contribution to the rescue operation would not be without risks. I saw Renata's eyes turn dark.

"What good is it that you die, too?" she shouted. "Does everybody have to panic?"

We were all torn up inside, and when I got back down after carrying up some medicine — my climb went without mishap — I sat in our mess tent with my head bowed. None of us had any appetite. We only sat there and listened to the voices outside.

Somewhere a helicopter was buzzing. I learned later that it was a Japanese TV crew. A Sherpa was shouting, and people were running back and forth, trying to find out the latest news, and at that moment, I couldn't hold down my thoughts any longer. It seemed like a sin toward those who right now were perishing on the mountain, but I couldn't help it.

"What will I do now?" I said. "Will my whole project go down the drain?"

I had gotten to be friends with the people who were dying up there, and it was excruciating to be down here and not be able to do anything. Even so, I had spent years preparing my expedition. This was the adventure of my life, and I couldn't bear the thought that it might be over. Or was it? Could I still climb up after the tumult had subsided? But what would people say about me if I climbed past those who had frozen to death?

Stuart Hutchison, a Canadian physician who was on Rob Hall's team, left Camp Four on the South Col on the morning of May 11 together with four Sherpas to look for his lost comrades. Quite soon—after having followed Anatoli's directions—the Sherpas found two bodies lying motionless in the snow, close to the edge of Everest's Kangshung Face. The first body—the smaller one—had a three-inch-thick layer of ice over the face. When Hutchison bent down in the howling wind at 26,200 feet and chipped the ice from the face, he recognized Yasuko Namba. She had lost both her gloves, and her hands were as hard as those of a mannequin. Her pupils were dilated and her skin was the color of white porcelain. To his horror, Hutchison saw that she was breathing.

"I was overwhelmed," he told Krakauer later. "I didn't know what to do."

Then he turned to Weathers. Weathers's face was also covered with a thick coating of ice, and there were balls of ice matted to his eyelids. Hutchison cleared it all off. Weathers mumbled something. It was like hearing a voice speak from the inside of a coffin.

"He was as close to death as a person can be and still be breathing," Hutchison related to Krakauer.

Stuart Hutchison turned to the Sherpas and asked for their advice.

Lhakpa Chhiri urged Hutchison to leave Weathers and Namba where they lay. He was a veteran in the business, respected for his good judgment, and his answer didn't mean that he was hard-hearted. In mountaineering, you have to concentrate your efforts on those who can be saved. You can't waste your energy on hopeless cases. Even if they managed to get Weathers and Namba to Camp Four, the Sherpa was sure they would die before they got to Base Camp.

What Hutchison didn't know was that something dreamlike was going on inside Weathers's head. Close to 5:00 P.M. the day before, Weathers had met Jon Krakauer, who was on his way down from the summit. Weathers was shivering in the cold and told Jon that he was waiting for Rob Hall to come back down.

Jon said it would take a long time for Rob to come. He asked Beck to come with him instead.

Weathers hesitated but decided to wait for Mike Groom, Rob's assistant guide. Groom came twenty minutes later, but by then, the sky had grown dark, and there was almost zero visibility because of the blowing snow—but this didn't really matter to Beck because he could barely see. Weathers joined Groom's group, but then everything degenerated into chaos. People were shouting and pummeling each other's backs to stay awake in the biting cold. Weathers slowly lost all feeling in his right hand, as he later told *People*. He took his glove off to warm his hand inside his jacket, but then the wind tore the glove out of his other hand, and it disappeared into the maelstrom.

Soon, all the voices around him became vague and strange, and after that, Beck Weathers didn't remember anything. Not Hutchison finding him, not mumbling something to Hutchison. He could only remember waking up suddenly, not knowing if he was dreaming or not.

"I was lying on my back in the ice," he recounted to *Newsweek*. "It was colder than anything you can believe. My right glove was gone, my hand looked like it was molded of plastic. . . . I could see the faces of my wife and children pretty clearly. I figured I had three or four hours left to live, so I started walking."

In Dallas, Beck Weathers's wife, Peach, had already received a phone call from Madeleine David, Rob Hall's assistant. She said she had terrible news. Peach Weathers didn't understand at first and asked if Beck was missing. Madeleine told her that he was dead.

Three hours afterward, the phone rang again. This time Peach was told that Beck was in critical condition but alive.

Not much later, the doorbell rang at Scott Fischer's home. It was 5:00 A.M., and Scott's wife, Jeannie Price, had been sleeping well, knowing that Scott had reached the summit and was doing fine. But now, in the early dawn, a small group of people stood outside her door: her sister, her brother-in-law, and Scott's best friend.

"It's Scott. . . . He's been hurt on the way down," her sister said, according to *Life*.

Soon her children were awakened by her crying.

Beck Weathers walked forward through the snowstorm across the South Col's stony wasteland. He saw hardly anything—it was all just a gray mist to him—and all the while, he was screaming in pain. The tissue of his body was dying from the cold. Those were the screams that guided Anatoli back to Camp Four. Then Weathers saw a strange rock. It looked smooth, but when he bumped up against it, something stood up.

"Rocks don't do that," was his reaction, he later told *Newsweek*.

At 4:35 P.M., the well-known American mountain guides Peter Athans and Todd Burleson—the advance guard of a general rescue operation—were camped on the South Col at 26,200 feet. Burleson had just gotten out of his tent when someone came walking toward him. He didn't believe his eyes; he shouted to Athans to come quick. The person held his right hand in front of him in a frozen, macabre salute, and Athans was reminded of a mummy in a low-budget horror film. Burleson realized it was Weathers, and they put him in a tent and gave him water and oxygen. Weathers had severe frostbite on his arms and black spots on his swollen face. His clothes were so stiff with ice that Burleson and Athans had to cut them off.

The hours passed. The evening came and then the night, and people in Camp Four had no time for tending to the frozen ghost of Beck Weathers. On the morning of May 12, most people in camp thought Weathers must have died during the night. His tent had been almost torn to pieces by the wind, and no one had heard a sound from him for a long time. Actually, Weathers was awake and shivering violently in the cold. During the night his sleeping bag had come off of him and he couldn't pull it back on. Instead he had screamed—but the hurricane stifled his voice.

"On top of everything else, my right arm was swelling up, and I had this stupid wristwatch on, so as my arm got bigger and bigger, the watch got tighter and tighter until it was cutting off most of the blood supply to my hand," Weathers says in Krakauer's book *Into Thin Air*.

That day, he was helped from the South Col all the way down to Camp Two by Athans and Burleson, filmmaker David Breashears, Ed Viesturs, and Veikka Gustafsson, among others. It must have taken a tremendous effort, and when he reached the camp, he was put in a tent together with the severely frostbitten Makalu Gau.

Attempts were made to get a Nepalese helicopter to come and pick up Weathers and Gau, but Camp Two was situated at 20,500 feet, and no rescue helicopter had ever landed at such an altitude before. The American Embassy finally persuaded the Nepalese Army to make the attempt. Lieutenant Colonel Madan Khatri Chhetri from Kathmandu took off in a helicopter that had been stripped of everything that wasn't essential and was as light as you could possibly make it. It also had hardly any spare gas onboard. Chhetri made two truly heroic trips above Base Camp, first picking up Gau, then Weathers, and flew them both to the hospital in Kathmandu.

The pilot later told *Newsweek* that Makalu Gau was laughing the whole way down at the thought of the thin margin by which he had cheated death.

Late at night on May 11, Rob Hall was still up on the mountain, a few hundred feet below the summit. It was incredible that he was still alive. Rob had summitted at 2:10 P.M. on May 10, then waited for almost two hours for forty-seven-year-old Doug Hansen to join him. It seemed to us inexplicable that Rob had let Doug summit that late in the day, because surely he must have understood that there was a reason why Hansen was taking so long. Rob had always been the rational one, but perhaps this time, for once, he'd let his emotions take over. When Doug approached the summit, Rob climbed down to meet him, put Doug's arm around his neck, and led him to the summit. Then they turned around.

At 4:30 P.M. on May 10, Rob called Base Camp to say that he and Doug were atop the Hillary Step—and they needed oxygen. He was told that there were two bottles waiting for them at the South Summit.

It was damned unfortunate that Andy Harris, Rob's assistant guide, overheard this conversation. Andy wouldn't live much longer. He was severely confused, even if he sounded sober and clearheaded. A little earlier, he'd told Jon Krakauer that the full oxygen bottles at the South Summit were empty, and now he repeated the same thing to Rob.

Because of this, Rob did not descend to retrieve the bottles. Instead he tried to get Doug down when neither man had any bottled oxygen left to breathe. This proved to be nearly impossible. By now Doug was in a severe state of exhaustion, and the two climbers were trapped at the end of the world as darkness came and the storm strengthened. At 5:36 P.M., Rob spoke on the radio to the New Zealand guide Guy Cotter, who was leading an expedition on the neighboring mountain, Pumori.

Cotter was a good friend of Rob's. He told Rob to leave Doug and continue down alone. "I know I sound like the bastard for telling Rob to abandon his client," Cotter later told Krakauer, "but by then it was obvious that leaving Doug was his only choice."

Rob probably could have made it down himself, but his promise to Doug was sacred; he wouldn't leave the summit without him. Exactly what happened during the hours that followed is not known. In a few radio conversations, Rob Hall expressed his concern about the rest of his clients. Then the radio went quiet. Shortly before 3:00 A.M., Guy Cotter awoke in his tent a couple of miles from Everest Base Camp. Words were pouring out of his radio. He heard someone saying, "Keep moving! Keep going!" while the storm howled in the background.

Guy Cotter thought it might be Rob's voice. He couldn't tell for sure, but probably he was right. Hall had a microphone strapped to his shoulder, and sometimes it got switched on by mistake. What Cotter heard was probably Rob's last attempts to get Doug Hansen down. He had been fighting for almost eleven hours and together they had gotten only a very short distance.

When Rob called Base Camp early in the morning of May 11, he was below the Hillary Step at the South Summit. He sounded confused. The physician Caroline Mackenzie talked with him.

He told her that his legs were strange and added: "I'm too clumsy to move."

"How is Doug?" Mackenzie asked.

"Doug is gone," Rob answered and broke off contact.

Rob never said what had happened to Doug. He never mentioned the postal worker again, and people in Base Camp didn't want to pressure him. They tried to be encouraging and to get him to start descending again and not to worry about his clients, but Rob kept asking how the others were doing. Beck? Andy? Yasuko?

When he called again, Rob said he was shivering furiously, but that the sun was rising over the mountain, and soon a faint ray of heat would reach the South Summit. In Base Camp, a small hope was ignited. "Perhaps someone can get up there and save him," people thought. But others knew what it was really like. Rob's wife, Jan Arnold, at her home in Christchurch, New Zealand, did.

Jan Arnold is a physician. She met Rob when she worked at a medical clinic for altitude-related illnesses in Pheriche, Nepal. On their very first date, Rob suggested that they climb together. Soon after, they scaled Cho Oyu in Nepal, then Vinson Massif, the tallest summit in Antarctica. In May 1993, they stood side by side on the top of Everest, and when Rob returned to the mountain in 1994 and 1995, Jan Arnold was the expedition physician. She was supposed to be their doctor this year, too, but now she was seven months pregnant with their first child, so Caroline Mackenzie had taken her place.

Jan Arnold was in Christchurch, but the satellite phone was hooked up to the radio, so she could talk to Rob. She tried to imagine a storm at close to 29,000 feet. She could visualize the summit in front of her. She had been there herself, and she knew that you can't really be rescued from a place like that, especially not after twelve hours without any bottled oxygen to breathe. At 5:00 A.M., Nepalese time, she talked with Rob for the first time. He was slurring his words. Jan said that he talked about all sorts of things. It was unbearable.

Later that morning, the Sherpas Ang Dorje and Lhakpa Chhiri made a heroic but unsuccessful attempt to rescue Rob. Meanwhile, Rob found the oxygen bottles at the South Summit that Andy Harris in his confusion had claimed were empty. Rob managed to get the ice off his oxygen mask, inhale the bottled air, and regain some of his power.

"I'm on my way down now," he said again and again, but he never got started.

He was thinking more clearly now, but his body wouldn't obey. His colleagues in Base Camp tried to talk him down, and finally he got annoyed. Krakauer quotes him as saying: "Look, if I thought I could manage the knots on the fixed ropes with my frostbitten hands, I would have gone down six hours ago, pal. Just send a couple of boys up with a big thermos of something hot—then I'll be fine."

Renata and I listened to the conversations from a dark green tent next to Rob Hall's well-equipped mess tent. They had a fax, some computer equipment, and a satellite phone. Everybody gathered there; this was where news about what was happening on the mountain came first.

A couple of kerosene lamps spread a peculiar light in the tent. Or were they solar cell powered lamps? I don't know. People in the corners looked like shadows, and sometimes the faint light fell on their faces. The room was as solemn and quiet as a church. People sat on plastic-covered air mattresses on the floor and hugged each other. Now and then someone cursed, while sometimes people whispered and mumbled to each other. This went on all day.

Renata and I walked in and out of the tent. Sometimes we got the feeling that we were witnessing something that was too horrible and too private—but we couldn't stay away. We needed to know what was going on, and I made a sketch of the mountain and marked the positions of the climbers. Others had already made similar maps, and mine didn't contribute much to the general knowledge, but what was I to do?

Slowly, the conversations with Rob changed in character. People gave him less advice about how to get down. Instead they just tried to divert him and to ease his pain.

"You think about that little baby of yours. You're going to see its face in a couple of months, so keep on going," Helen Wilton said. Others told Rob to move or to massage his body to restore circulation.

"Do you remember how much fun we had in Indonesia?" someone else asked him, and finally a certain warmth, a guy-to-guy feeling, entered the conversation.

Later, when Rob didn't answer, people got more worried.

Soon we understood that Rob's hands were destroyed. He could no longer tell if he had pressed the send button on the radio. At 6:20 P.M., his last phone call came. Some say that a few radio stations broadcast this final conversation. In any case, Guy Cotter talked to Rob Hall and told him that Jan Arnold was on the line.

"Give me a minute," Rob said. "Me mouth's dry. I want to eat a bit of snow before I talk to her."

Then he heard her.

"I can't tell you how much I'm thinking about you," she said. "Are you warm, my darling?"

"In the context of the altitude, the setting, I'm reasonably comfortable," he answered.

"How are your feet?"

"I haven't taken me boots off to check, but I think I may have a bit of frostbite. . . ."

"I'm looking forward to making you completely better when you come home."

"I hope you're tucked up in a nice warm bed."

They talked for a while about what they were going to name their baby. Then Jan said: "Don't feel that you're alone. I'm sending all my positive energy your way."

"I love you," Rob said. "Sleep well, my sweetheart. Please don't worry too much."

"See you," she said.

12

THE SURVIVORS BEGAN
heading home. Base Camp was breaking up. It felt like we alone
were being left behind. Time had run away from us. It wouldn't be
long now until the monsoon hit, and then my chances of reaching
Everest's summit would disappear with the falling rain. The other
day, Helen Wilton had come over to our mess tent. She looked
stressed and confused.

"Do you need anything?" she asked, as if the catastrophe had
hit us, not her.

"No," we said. Then she whirled around talking about everything she had to remember, but suddenly she grew pale and passed
out. When Helen came to again, she wept.

"This didn't happen. It can't be true," she said.

When we tried to comfort her, she told us it was her birthday.

"Now I can never celebrate my birthday again. It's all so horrible. I haven't called my kids yet. I want to, but what am I supposed to tell them?"

Now Helen had departed for home and her kids, but she'd
left her feelings of emptiness and despair for us to deal with. It was

like being at a vacation spot after all the visitors have left. All joy is gone, and what remains is gravity and a fear that the days are passing too quickly. Magnus and Fredrik had left, too, and I could sense that Renata also wanted to leave—even though she didn't really want to. We both knew that it would be unbearable for me to return home without having tried for the summit a second time. But no one thought I would make it. I could sense it. But I was used to that, and it gave me strength. I got to be the underdog.

Journalists called. Jennet Conant—wife of the *60 Minutes* star Steve Kroft—was representing *Vanity Fair,* and she wanted to know about Sandy Pittman.

Many people have vouched for her good character, including David Breashears, who time and again has defended her approach to climbing. It's also true that Sandy was in very good physical shape and that she was by no means the least experienced climber on the mountain. But there were so many examples of her arrogance. In the village of Pheriche below Base Camp, to get to Kathmandu as quickly as possible after the tragedy, she chartered a helicopter for over $2,000 and offered Tim Madsen and the physician Ingrid Hunt a ride. For the same price, she could have gotten a Russian helicopter and given everybody in her expedition a ride—those who saved her life, for instance.

Scott Fischer's death was partly caused by the fact that he burned himself out helping inexperienced climbers, like Pittman, ascend the mountain. Sandy made it back down alive because Neal Beidleman and Anatoli Boukreev led the way and even carried her. Still, she didn't mention either one of them in her long talks with *Newsweek* and NBC TV. When she was asked in a later interview why she didn't thank the men who had saved her life, she had to ask, according to *Vanity Fair,* which two gentlemen they were referring to.

It's sad. Rob and Scott died because they felt deeply committed to the amateurs that they were guiding. Still, Sandy insisted that there were no heroes in this drama.

Some people choose Everest for their first climb. Some have barely practiced on a little rock back home first. As for myself, I'd paid my dues before I went up on an 8,000-meter peak. I made my mistakes on smaller mountains. I scaled Pik Lenin, Muztagh Tower, Pik Pobeda, Cho Oyu, K2, and Broad Peak before I came here. I lived in a gravel pit, I studied hard, and I trained like crazy. Still, I'm not immune to danger. No climber in the world is safe on Mount Everest. Sagarmatha, Chomolungma, cannot be conquered.

Many people believe that they are safe with mountain guides. They hand over all personal responsibility to them, and they don't even realize that climbing on your own with a friend or climbing partner—and being taken care of by a daddy on the mountain—are two completely different things.

Many people also climb for the sake of publicity rather than for the experiences of joy it brings them. I want publicity, too—I live on it—but what drives me is the love of the mountains and of adventure, and it pains me to see Everest and other high peaks reduced to trophies kept in a china cabinet. Because "collecting" these sacred mountains poisons the air up here.

The commercial circus on Mount Everest keeps growing, and that increases the risks. David Breashears, the filmmaker, was the first professional mountaineer to guide a client, his friend the multimillionaire Dick Bass, to the summit of Everest in 1985. Bass was fifty-five at the time, and he became the oldest person to reach the summit. As I've said before, Dick Bass was also—along with the Norwegian Arne Naess—the first of the super-rich to be ushered to the top of the world. But back then, eleven years ago, Breashears and Bass had Everest almost to themselves. They stood alone on the summit and gazed out over the vast wilderness. Now, there's rush-hour traffic on the mountain. According to many who were there, the major reason why things got slowed down on May 10 was because there were simply too many people following the same route, while time ticked relentlessly by.

Even though Rob Hall and Scott Fischer in many ways deserve praise, they are not entirely without blame for creating this sideshow on Everest. Because of the big money in guided ascents, the guides (who usually start out as financially strapped climbers) often can't bring themselves to turn away a wealthy client who really shouldn't be on the mountain. In an interview in *Life,* Edmund Hillary says that he once met one of Rob Hall's clients, a guy who had hardly any climbing experience at all. The man was willing to pay tens of thousands of dollars, and Rob accepted him. Why? Because of the money? Because of Rob's overconfidence in his own ability as a guide?

Edmund Hillary has also said that the increasing commercialization of Everest makes people lose their respect for the mountain, and that's dangerous. You have to fear Mount Everest to survive Mount Everest, and no one can buy a guarantee to survive — not even for $65,000. The money makes people take unnecessary risks. What was it really that happened up there that year? Two of the world's best guides decided to disregard the rule not to pursue the summit after 2:00 P.M. Would Rob Hall have let Doug Hansen reach the summit so dangerously late in the day if Hansen hadn't paid him so much money? I don't know. Rob often said, in a voice that was almost solemn, that you had to have as much respect for the clock as you had for the mountain.

"I will tolerate no dissension up there," Krakauer also quotes Rob as saying to his clients before they went up. "My word will be absolute law, beyond appeal. If you don't like a particular decision I make, I'd be happy to discuss it with you afterward, but not while we're on the hill."

Still, he gave no order to his clients to turn around. Instead, he sat at the highest point in the world until 4:00 P.M., waiting for a client who saw Everest as the goal of his dreams. It may sound beautiful, but it was—with due respect to Rob—madness.

Probably the competition between the two guides also played a part. Rob had guided thirty-nine people to the summit and was the king of the business, but this year he had competition from a man who charged just as much as he did and who lived in the U.S., where most of the ultra-rich clients are. On top of that, Scott had a face that worked well on talk shows and in ads. Rob witnessed all of Scott's clients summit, including Sandy Pittman, while several of his own gave up. Perhaps that was part of the reason why Rob stayed and waited for Doug Hansen.

There have been ads for commercial expeditions claiming "100% Everest Success." But how can you honestly write that, knowing that the mountain has claimed more than 150 lives? Ian McNaught-Davis, president of the International Mountaineering and Climbing Federation, thinks that nowadays we should try to impart cowardice rather than courage in the hearts of amateur climbers. He thinks that anyone who has not scaled other 8,000-meter peaks should not be allowed to climb Everest, and he is right.

Many people might laugh at the superstitions of the Sherpa people, who see every storm on the mountain as Everest's revenge or the wrath of a god. Perhaps you can ridicule some of their beliefs, but I, too, sense a strange, primordial force when I'm high in the Himalaya, and I think it's healthy to consider Everest as a living being. That way, you are alert to the moodiness of the mountain; your respect for nature increases, and so does your margin of safety.

It might sound like I'm trying to be a wise guy. I know I have many shortcomings, too, and not long ago, I was balancing on a very thin line between life and death. It's very easy to have 20-20 vision in hindsight, and perhaps it might just as well have been the other way around: me in a snowdrift up on the mountain, and Rob and Scott hailed as heroes. Perhaps they would have criticized me.

But I still want to be the opposite of Sandy Pittman and all of her peers; I want to be their antithesis. I wanted to make it to the summit on my own, without using bottled oxygen. I didn't want to litter the mountain with my empty oxygen cylinders. And more important, I don't want to hide anything, either—and that's why I have to admit openly that now, after the tragedy, I had to modify my principles. I began to eat food prepared by our Base Camp cook. I had no choice. I was worn out, I had to build myself back up in order to somehow try to make another attempt—even though I had my doubts I could. Everest, the mountain, still felt full of anger; we could hear the jet stream roaring. I wondered if there would be any more decent weather this season.

Most of the Sherpas had lost the spark in their eyes. They were downhearted and worried and wanted to go home. Probably they wondered on whom Chomolungma would seek revenge the next time. I understood them. On May 9, the Taiwanese Chen Yu-Nan had died on the mountain. On the tenth and eleventh, Andy Harris, Rob Hall, Doug Hansen, Scott Fischer, Yasuko Namba, and the Indian climbers Tsewang Smanla, Tsewang Paljor, and Dorje Morup had died. Back home in Dallas, Beck Weathers had to have his right arm amputated, and he lost all five fingers on his left hand. The doctors cut off his nose and made him a new one. His face, I heard, was still covered with black spots—souvenirs from his visit to the kingdom of the dead. And he was plagued by nightmares. Still, he has experienced moments of euphoria since his rescue, and he has understood the great miracle of being alive.

I and the rest of the Westerners who were still in Base Camp hesitated for a long time before we acknowledged that we wanted to try for the summit again, in spite of what had happened. Even some members of the IMAX team—which had a $5.5-million budget—

thought it was time to pack up and go home. But in the end, every-body stayed. During the days, we listened to reports from meteoro-logical institutes all over the world, and then we compared their forecasts. We knew that the climbing season was running out. We had to find another window when the jet stream was no longer howling and before the heavy monsoon snowfall began.

On May 17, when I left Base Camp and set off again into the Icefall, another fatality occurred on the mountain—as if there hadn't been enough. The Austrian Reinhard Wlasich, climbing without bottled oxygen, reached the high camp on the Tibetan side. Inside the tent, he felt sick. Soon he fell unconscious and died, after probably suffering both cerebral and pulmonary edema.

Jesus and I and several other climbers—among them the IMAX film team and the South Africans—were all en route to Camp Four. The nervousness in Base Camp amplified. Renata, our Sherpa cook, and all our Sherpa staff were getting irritable and restless.

Suddenly, Renata heard a disquieting crash outside her tent. She rushed out and saw that the wooden pole in our Base Camp altar had fallen over! To the Sherpas, this was just about the worst sign that a climber could have.

"Now we're headed for disaster," Renata thought. Even a sensible woman like her could become superstitious after five weeks in Base Camp. The locals informed her that you needed to burn a special kind of incense to remedy the damage, but there was no incense like that around. Instead, Renata and our Sherpas burned whatever they could find—baskets, twigs—in an attempt to placate the mountain gods. She didn't tell any of this to me, which was good. The howl coming from the summit was omi-nous enough.

13

THE JET STREAM ROARED like warplanes. Jesus and I sat in a tent that the Taiwanese had left behind at Camp Four. My own tent, which stood 300 vertical feet farther down, had been blown away in the storm of May 10 and 11. So we were forced to stay in the Taiwanese camp. There was a drawing of a rhinoceros on the tent's ceiling. Each blast of wind hitting the tent made the rhino flutter as if it were having severe spasms. Jesus had pulled his yellow, hooded jacket snugly around his evenly tanned face and trimmed beard. I had been badly sunburned. Skin was peeling off my red and bloated nose, which made me look like an alcoholic. For some time now, I had also been suffering from a severe dry cough, which tore at my chest. I felt lethargic, still weak, and honestly speaking, I was starting to lose hope. Jesus shook his head in doubt, too. His breaths came hard and heavily.

"Very many windows," he said. It took me a while before I understood what he meant.

"Oh," I finally answered. "You mean, 'very many winds,'" as if the extra syllable was the only linguistic error in his sentence. My

Spanish was poor, Jesus's English was even worse, and we certainly weren't exchanging many profound thoughts. But we were experienced climbers, and some things could be communicated without words. After all, we didn't need to talk to know that the wind was still blowing.

"It's not at all certain that we'll reach the summit tomorrow," I spoke into my camcorder. Still, this was the best weather we'd had in a long time. "I hope the jet stream won't hit us, because then the tent will blow away and I'll go with it," I joked, stumbling over my words. Then I added, in a half-crazy mood: "But that's all right," and I winked with my left eye at the camera.

It was almost comical. I looked like a complete wreck, I sounded like a ghost—and I was deeply worried. Still, somehow I winked and joked and feigned being in a good humor. I opened the tent door and shot a sequence of the South Summit, which reached high above us into the sky, then I let the camera travel horizontally across all the green oxygen bottles lying on the stony ground near us, over a couple of body bags, and to a gray tent that was about to collapse in the wind. A hell of a place, the South Col of Everest.

"I've never seen anything like it," I said, again looking into my camcorder. My voice was sounding desperate.

Everest did not want me up there. After two terrible days stuck in Camp Four, we returned to Camp Two at an altitude of 20,500 feet. Here we met Ang Rita, the IMAX team, and the Frenchman Tierry Renard. Tierry was a bearded, somewhat hairy man who'd been on long journeys in South America. One time he encountered—so he claimed—an Indian tribe whose tradition prescribed that the father cut his son's umbilical cord, then climb up a high mountain and place the cord at the summit—to bring luck to the child. Terry liked this tradition, so much that now he was going to climb Mount Everest to put the umbilical cord from his own child at the top. He had the cord safely stored in a jar in his backpack.

David Breashears, leader of the IMAX team, was in Camp Two with eight Sherpas. He said that two days from now we would probably have the best weather we'd had in a long time. As for myself, I became more and more aware of how tired I was. My last two days at Camp Four waiting for a break in the weather had been more taxing than I realized — and I knew now that if I didn't climb back up when the good weather came, then I might as well pack my things and go home. If I went up, it would be my third attempt without supplemental oxygen in a three-week period. Not many people had tried that.

"For good reason, perhaps," I thought to myself.

We all decided to try to reach the summit on May 23, and I arranged with Ang Rita that he carry my camcorder up the mountain. But he would bring nothing else belonging to me or for me. This might sound like yet one more deviation from my principles, but the camcorder, I reasoned, wasn't necessary for the climb. It had to be brought only to record images as evidence.

Ang Rita, Jesus, and I crowded together and slept in a tent made for two. Things were all over the place, and for a couple of hours I dozed with my head on top of a saucepan. All the while, the storm raged outside. But I knew it must eventually subside. It had to!

On the morning of May 21, we set off again from Camp Two.

"This is the last chance," I told the camcorder. "And we're going to take it."

Meanwhile, Renata was suffering from rheumatic problems for the first time in her life. Apart from that, though, she'd been holding up quite well in Base Camp. For a while, she'd joked about being homesick. Now she'd stopped joking. She'd had enough, and she desperately wanted me to reach the summit so we could get out of there. Before I'd left for the Icefall this last time, she gave me a short hug and uttered a short, "Bye!" — as if she didn't dare to let our leave-taking last longer than that. She was afraid, I suppose, of not being able to let go of me. We both knew the stakes, and the catastrophe of May 10 and 11 lay between us like a wall. We didn't mention it, but it was there all the same. Worry rested heavily on her, I could tell.

Then, after I turned back at Camp Four because of the continued bad weather, the Sherpas at Base Camp walked around with an expression that told her: "We told you so, didn't we? The mountain is angry. No one else will make it to the top this year."

Now I was climbing up at the same time as the IMAX team, and Base Camp was more deserted than ever. Everyone felt we were climbing on borrowed time, that the season should have ended by now. I knew that I could challenge the mountain only this one last time.

On the night of May 22, the stars shone brightly in the sky. Renata moved her sleeping bag into our mess tent. Usually, she didn't sleep in here, but tonight she wanted to be close to the radio, which stood next to an old, rusty table and a couple of folding chairs. There was no light in the tent, so Renata put her headlamp on her head and lay staring into the darkness, waiting for a sound to come from the radio.

During the weeks she'd spent in Base Camp, she'd read a lot — Tolkien's *The Lord of the Rings* trilogy, among other books. But tonight, she wasn't going to read or sleep. "It doesn't feel right," she thought to herself, "to sleep when Göran is on the mountain. My thoughts should be with him," and in her mind she listed all of the reasons why this time I should be able to make it.

"It's a good thing Ang Rita is with him," she concluded. "He's been to the summit nine times, so the mountain god has to like him at least." Renata knew that we ought to leave the South Col at midnight. She looked at the clock again and again, and every time the radio crackled, she jumped. A couple of times she heard other voices, but never mine. The night became painfully long and silent. It felt like an eternity. Still, she was afraid of the approaching morning. She was afraid dawn would come before she'd heard anything from me.

At 5:00 A.M. the radio crackled again. She jumped up and hit her knee against a chair, but quickly grabbed hold of the radio and called: "Göran, over!"

"I'm at 27,900 feet," I rattled out.

"How is it going?"

"Cold; hard!"

"Are you going to the top?"

"I'll keep climbing."

The conversation was cut off, and Renata's stomach started to ache. She was so nervous she began to feel sick. She paced up and down, waiting to hear from me again. The minutes passed. For a moment she believed she heard footsteps outside. Or was it in her imagination that she heard someone walking by? She shrugged off the thought. She thought about the small Japanese woman, Namba, who'd sat beside her at Rob Hall's party. Now she lay dead, her frozen body still up on the South Col. It was all so surreal.

"Göran! Göran! What are you doing?!"

The radio crackled back. She heard something, a faint panting, but she didn't even know if it was me. Perhaps it was somebody who'd turned on his radio by mistake and just happened to end up on our frequency.

"Göran, if that is you," she shouted, "don't bother about the radio. Don't waste your energy on it. Just climb!"

Then there was only silence. At six in the morning, she lapsed into despair. Had something really serious happened to us? Still, she didn't wake anybody up—due to her consideration for others which not even her fear could shake. At 7:00 A.M., the sun rose above Base Camp and the Icefall. Not until 8:30 did she dart into the tent of one of the South Africans remaining down here.

"I haven't heard from Göran in hours. Do you think something has happened to him?"

"Eh . . . ?" the man said drowsily and turned over in his sleeping bag to look at her. The fear in Renata's face didn't register with him.

"I'm a bit slow in the mornings," he answered. "Umm, could you come back in twenty minutes?"

"Okay, sorry," Renata said vacantly.

She went outside. She cursed. She walked briskly, then suddenly she ran over the rocks and moraine toward the IMAX team's tent, hardly knowing what she was doing. Their Base Camp manager, Paula Barton Viesturs, also had been up for a long time. She was pouring herself a cup of tea when Renata came rushing toward her.

Paula asked in a kind voice: "Would you like a cup?"

Renata shook her head and asked: "How are they doing?"

"Good! They are on their way to the summit," Paula answered innocently.

"Have you heard anything about Göran? I haven't heard from him in four hours," Renata said, making an effort to hide her nervousness.

She didn't succeed very well. Her words conjured up a tangled skein of emotions. Paula was as empathetic as she could be, under the circumstances, and expressed her concern.

"You don't need to worry," she answered, but this didn't quiet Renata's fears. She still felt a sense of dread clutching at her that wouldn't release its stranglehold. The atmosphere had altered so dramatically from my first summit attempt. And Paula seemed to be worried, Renata thought, that today another climber might run into trouble, and that the IMAX team would have to carry out yet another rescue mission.

"Haven't we rescued enough people?" Paula seemed to be thinking.

Renata's cheeks flushed with anxiety, but she responded, trying to sound calm: "You're probably right. He's probably turned off the radio and is concentrating on the climb."

She walked away from the IMAX tent. The hours passed, and at 10:00 A.M., Renata was told that the Frenchman Tierry had summitted with his umbilical cord. Two hours later, she was told that the IMAX team had reached the top, too. "But where is Göran?" she wondered, ever more desperately. "Where is he?"

At 1:00 P.M. she talked over the radio with Jamling Tenzing Norgay.

Jamling Norgay is the middle son of Tenzing Norgay, Hillary's partner on that first Everest ascent. Jamling grew up in Darjeeling where his father had settled, and he learned to climb with his dad. Now he was one of the star climbers in David Breashears's IMAX film project. Being Tenzing's son, he could thank his father—a national hero in India and Nepal—for a large part of his success.

Jamling Norgay was heading down after reaching the summit when he gave Renata, if not the worst, then at least the next-to-worst information she could have received.

"I think Göran turned around," he said, hesitating slightly. "I don't think he made it."

The possibility of my defeat rushed through Renata's mind.

"No, no, no," she thought. "What will I tell people back home? How will I explain it?"

I reached Camp Four at 7:00 P.M.—extremely late in the day. Ang Rita, Jesus, and I again crept into the Taiwanese tent. I supposed that Makalu Gau had sat in here, too, the night before May 10, when he climbed to the summit and then nearly died. What would it be like for us tomorrow, I wondered?

None of us had the strength to talk. We just sat around and made some food. Every little movement was hard work and required an enormous effort. Only Ang Rita was holding up relatively well. As for myself, I'd suffered a severe case of diarrhea during the previous night and had lost a lot of liquid.

I switched on my camcorder. At first there was only darkness. Then Jesus came into focus and said, "Hola," in a ghostly voice. Ang Rita looked morosely at the camera, as if thinking that this was all just Western nonsense. I'd rolled up my balaclava cap so that my straggly hair peeked out from under it. My beard had grown thick and turned surprisingly red.

"I'm totally exhausted, I'm gone," I wheezed out to the camcorder. Then I went on: "In five hours, I'm going to take my backpack and all the stuff and ascend 4,900 vertical feet to the top. It'll be very interesting. It will take will, will, will."

I switched off the camcorder, and with my last strength took off my jacket and several layers of underwear. This might seem strange—as it was bitterly cold in the tent—but if you wear too much clothing while in your sleeping bag, then you'll sweat and you'll be more likely to get frostbitten the next day. The most important thing, I'd learned, was to change your socks and keep them dry. When I tried to climb Everest on May 3 and turned back at the South Summit, I'd had problems with my toes. Now I tended to them as if they were newborn babies. I gave them a massage.

Then I lay down, pulled up my sleeping bag, and closed my eyes. I listened to Jesus and Ang Rita breathe, heard the wind rustle, and then everything merged into a strange picture. I fell asleep and slept relatively well, even if I woke up now and then, and felt some agony of death as I gasped for breath in the thin, cold air. When the alarm clock went off shortly before midnight, I felt as if I'd slept for only a couple of minutes. I sat up and looked around. "What a mess," I thought.

There were clothes, pots, and oxygen bottles everywhere. We'd put the empty bottles inside the tent on purpose, to weigh it down so the tent wouldn't blow away in the storm. I rummaged through the heaps, looking for my clothes. It was intensely cold. I started to shiver. Ang Rita was already outside. He'd gathered some snow and now he sat at the tent opening, melting the snow in a pot on our stove. When he was done, I mixed several quarts of apricot and blueberry soup. I ate only some nuts; I couldn't get anything else down. But I drank as if there was no way I could ever quench my thirst. I could see that Ang Rita was getting impatient.

"We must go," he said firmly.

"Just a minute," I answered. "I have to drink." I knew that if I was going to survive the day, I had to restore my fluid balance, and I kept forcing down the blue soup.

We left camp for the summit at 12:54 A.M. It was pitch dark out, a special kind of darkness with a bluish tint, and far away I could see the IMAX team's headlamps roving around in the darkness. But it was quiet! I could hardly hear the jet stream. Listening to the crunching sound of my crampons biting into the snow as I climbed, I drifted slowly off into my own world, isolated from the others. But at that moment, my religious doubts intruded. I often got them at high altitude.

"Will this work? Is there anybody up here helping me?" I thought.

I recalled that during his solo ascent of Everest in 1980, Reinhold Messner felt the presence of an invisible companion at his side, and I began thinking about all the unearthly visions climbers have had up here on Everest's upper slopes and of the strange things that had happened to me on K2.

Then it occurred to me that Scott ought to be lying somewhere around here. I tried to shrug off the thought. I didn't want to see him, I didn't want to be reminded of what happened – but when I looked off to my right, there he was, entangled in a rope, frozen in an unfathomable motion. His face was covered with snow, and I couldn't help thinking: "What the hell, Scott? What happened?"

I hurried on. Soon I found myself in deep snow. The climbing was getting tough. Below, Jesus and Ang Rita were catching up to me, and above, the IMAX team climbers disappeared out of sight ahead of me. I was slowing down. I got scared.

"Göran," I muttered to myself. "What's three times three?

"Nine.

"Six plus seven?

"Wait a little . . . Thirteen, damn it!

"Yes, I can still think. At least so far. Or perhaps I just believe that I'm still in full possession of my faculties—don't all lunatics believe that?" I went on thinking like that. I tested myself in various ways, and I wondered how cerebral edema actually began. "Do I have any symptoms yet?"

I passed by more dead bodies and body bags. I could feel myself getting increasingly tired.

Soon Jesus and Ang Rita passed me, and I started feeling like I was dying of exhaustion. "Have I ever been this tired before?" I asked myself, and when I'd at last gotten above the point where I'd turned back on my first summit attempt, I could no longer walk more than six or seven steps at a time. Finally, I sat down in the snow to rest. I put my head on my ice axe and mumbled, "I'm in such a miserable state." Then I looked up.

Heaven was strange! It was covered with blue, yellow, and red stars. They danced around like a light show! Then I panicked. "No, no—I've gotten cerebral edema," I said, and in a flash I remembered what happened to Daniel Bidner on K2. First he saw small red houses and flags. Then he fell down a precipice and died.

"I have to turn back. What a damn pity, but I have to get back down. I will only rest a little first."

But when I cautiously raised my head again and looked up at the mountain, the stars were gone. I saw only the white reality of the snow slopes. I decided to continue.

"Go on! Go on! Brace yourself!"

Far below me, the tents at Camp Four now looked like small yellow dots. I was at 28,500 feet, and I climbed along the upper Southeast Ridge toward the South Summit. I knew that any moment now I would see the main summit, too. After a while, I turned on my camcorder and said tersely, panting:

"There's the top. I'm scared. Mommy! Let me live for another ten hours. The view is absolutely incredible. Lhotse, Kangchenjunga, Makalu." I was whispering in a tormented and barely audible voice. The mountains all around me were sticking up through the clouds below me. Then I saw him. He lay in a snowdrift. His right hand was bare and swollen and looked like it was holding onto an invisible radio, as if Rob were still talking to his wife Jan at home in New Zealand. There were lots of oxygen bottles around him, and I noticed that he'd taken off his crampons.

The ridge was only two or three yards wide. I had to climb right over him. As I did this, I thought—even though I hardly had the energy to think—that if you freeze to death, at least you die feeling warm, because at the very end, the body opens up the veins and pumps the blood out to the skin.

Soon after I crested the South Summit, I met the IMAX film team climbers, who had been to the top and were on their way down. As I looked at them, I felt terribly vulnerable. In their oxygen masks and wearing their other equipment, they looked like extraterrestrials, and for a moment, I thought they were just another hallucination. Ever since I'd seen the multicolored stars in the sky, I was no longer so sure about reality. And now I seriously doubted what my eyes saw. Imagine: Here I came panting up the ridge, without bottled oxygen or anything to help me breathe, and there they stood with their dark masks and oxygen bottles, each looking exactly the same—like ten identical Darth Vaders. The only thing missing was the hovering spaceship.

"Don't push too hard," one of them told me.

"No, I won't," I wheezed, as if suffering from consumption.

I was approaching the Hillary Step, but I didn't feel any excitement or positive expectations. I only wanted to get to the damned top and back down in safety, to Renata, and to collapse on a cot. Ahead of me were lots of ropes. I was so tired; I wondered which ones I should hold on to. But then I recalled, in a haze, my ambition to reach the summit without using any other people's ropes and ladders, and I remember old bleached ropes I'd seen on other mountains that had broken or were as weak as life itself here, so I climbed up the Hillary Step without touching them. If I took a single false step, it would be my last one. I was careful, and I didn't slip. Then somebody came along, descending. It was Jesus, on his way down from the summit. He was trembling like an aspen leaf, shivering with cold.

"How much farther?" I asked.

"At your pace, fifteen, twenty minutes," he said, and we parted.

I continued upward. "I'm going to get there, I'm going to get there," I repeated over and over to myself, and now it was only seven, six, five, four yards left, and there was Ang Rita, at the top for the tenth time, and he greeted me. There I stood, one foot in Nepal, the other in Tibet. I was at the top of the world and I could see other giant mountains, and all of them were now below me.

"I made it!" I cried deliriously, in a strange, cracked voice. "I made it. Yes! I'm totally exhausted. Wonder if I'll make it back down. I made it. Hell! I'm only halfway."

My lips were blue-black. My beard was covered with hoarfrost. Around me in the snow were prayer flags, locks of hair, photographs, ice axes, and all sorts of things climbers had placed here as remembrances when they reached the top. The summit itself was no larger than a snowdrift. We took a few pictures, and I talked incessantly into the camcorder. Even if I was happy to be here—or realized that I ought to be happy—mostly I was very, very scared.

"Now I have to ride my bike all the way home, too. If I'm still alive then," I said, then continued: "I only want to get down now. I don't dare stay any longer. Now I'm going down. I hope I'll survive," and off I staggered, followed by Ang Rita.

"Concentrate!" I mumbled to myself as I took one careful step at a time, but the descent down the Hillary Step went dreamlike and slow, and suddenly I fell. Luckily my crampons got entangled in a rope, and I stopped, hanging upside down at the edge of the world—but I didn't panic. My senses were so numb, and I was so set on getting down, that I just started methodically disentangling myself and continued descending.

Then I saw Rob Hall again. I took pictures of him. His face, though, was completely covered with snow. Next to his frozen hand was an ice axe and something else, maybe a down jacket. Was Doug Hansen lying under the snow, too? I don't know. I didn't want to know. I hurried along over the South Summit, then sat down in the snow and slid. But then the slope steepened, and with an increasing risk of avalanches, I stood up and stumbled down.

At 27,600 feet, I stopped to photograph Scott. Then I collapsed. The IMAX team passed by me. Now I could take only one step at a time, and I felt more exhausted than I ever thought was possible. Suddenly something turned on inside of me. I desperately tried to pull my pants down, but I had diarrhea, I couldn't stop it. Then I lost my balance and fell into a small crevasse right when the shit was running out of me.

What misery.

All through the afternoon, Renata continued to get conflicting information, and several journalists from Sweden called her.

"I don't know," she told them, feeling more and more dejected. "I don't know if Göran made it to the top."

"It's a bit like the Academy Awards," she thought. "Will I win? Won't I win? But it's much worse, because here it is a matter of life and death." She suspected that it wasn't true that I had turned around, but she didn't know anything for sure, and it was already 4:00 P.M. Surely, she ought to have heard from me by now! At that moment, she heard a voice outside the tent. It was Paula Barton Viesturs from the IMAX team.

"Yes?" Renata said. "What's happened?"

"We think Göran made it to the top."

Renata shuddered but tried to stay calm. She told herself that she still didn't know for sure. She picked up a camcorder and ran with Paula to the IMAX team's tent, and grabbed one of their radios.

"Did Göran make it to the top?" she asked, when she made contact with David Breashears.

Silence. Then she heard only: "I don't know."

"Do I have to go crazy? Will I never get an answer?" she shouted and whirled about with flushing cheeks. Then our trekking agent, Woungchu Sherpa, came up to her. He looked at Renata in a knowing way, then pushed back his hair from his forehead.

"Göran and Ang Rita were at the summit together," he said.

"What?"

"Göran made it. Congratulations! He made it."

Then Renata cried out. It was a cry that came from deep inside her, as several months of tension suddenly dissolved. She ran around and hugged everybody, feeling as if she wanted to call the whole world, and tell everyone, and that's what she did, more or less. On the satellite phone, she got hold of Gerard, my dad, who was in Zagreb.

"He made it!" she shouted.

"Is it true?" Gerard asked.

"Yes!" she screamed.

But there were many things that Renata still didn't know. Renata imagined that I'd been standing on the summit, reaching my arms up, as though I'd just scored the winning goal in the World Cup final. She believed that I must be overwhelmed with joy. She didn't realize that I hardly cared if I survived, that I was existing in a timeless vacuum, and that I stank. My face was blue, and it was very hard for me to breathe. I lay in the tent at Camp Four on the South Col hocking up phlegm and parts of my throat, totally exhausted. How did I make it down the last part of the route to where I am now, I wondered? I really didn't know. And I certainly didn't have the energy to talk. When Jamling Norgay came up to me, looking like he wanted to ask me something, I just waved him off.

"He's in Camp Four now," Paula Barton Viesturs said to Renata. "You can talk to him."

Renata brightened up as she got ready to shout congratulations into the receiver, but Jamling Norgay, not me, was on the other end and stated flatly: "He doesn't want to talk to you."

"Doesn't he? Perhaps he didn't make it to the top after all," she thought emotionally. "Or is he angry with me?"

My night was horrible. I still suffered from diarrhea and I coughed up greenish-black clots of phlegm. My bronchi were gone. I couldn't talk even if I wanted to. I was in the South Africans' tent, and an oxygen bottle was lying next to me. No, I was not going to use it — but it was comforting to know it was there.

Dawn arrived. Jesus shook me and made sure that I was awake. The sleeping pad that I'd borrowed from the South Africans was covered with the contents of my bowels. I took great pains to clean it. Then I drank. I downed a tremendous amount of liquid, trying to restore my hydration. When I finally got outside to begin my descent, the sunlight made my eyes hurt. I zigzagged between empty oxygen bottles, rocks, and ripped and abandoned tents. I felt absolutely, totally, one hundred percent completely and utterly wrecked. I couldn't keep up with Ang Rita or Jesus. My legs were extremely shaky and they almost refused to obey me. Soon I met Bruce Harrod, who at that point didn't know that he had only one more day to live.

"We're heading up for the summit tomorrow," he told me.

"Good luck," I coughed, then kept going. It was five degrees above zero Fahrenheit. A little later, I fell to my knees and let my head sink down to my ice axe. It took a while before I noticed some climbers from the IMAX team were standing near me.

"I can manage," I whispered hoarsely and got back up. I listened indifferently to a conversation between the team's leader, David Breashears, and a woman in Base Camp.

"He seems to be getting weaker and weaker. I'll probably stay here with him for a while and see how he does," David spoke into his radio.

Then I got it. They were talking about me. And that made me mad. Somehow I managed to make my legs move and I reeled down to Camp Three, where Ang Rita had prepared some crackers and pieces of meat for me to eat. My stomach protested. I started walking again, and when I came to the Lhotse Face, I got caught in a shower of stones. It was 1:00 P.M. It had been approximately twenty-four hours since I'd stood on the summit, and I still had a fair ways to go to reach Base Camp.

Then I saw a couple of larger stones bouncing in my direction—in fact straight toward me—and I had to jump with both feet together so as not to be hit. A group of Sherpas was 150 feet below me. There was a light mist over the mountain; I couldn't really see them—and they couldn't see the falling rocks. I tried to scream a warning to them, but my voice didn't project. I could manage only a hoarse whisper, but a few minutes later, when I learned my Sherpa friends were okay, I thanked the mountain gods that the stones had missed them.

We slept in Camp Two, Ang Rita, Jesus, and I. I was still too hoarse and weak to speak. I simply lay there with my own excrement dried on my clothes. It was pure humiliation, and before I fell asleep, I wondered, almost indifferently, if I had enough strength left to make it to Base Camp. Would I really be able to negotiate the Icefall?

The next day, we dismantled our campsite and left. Immediately, I lagged far behind the others, and when I reached the top of the Icefall, I saw that my fears were true. Summer was nearly here. The warm weather had turned the snow into a coarse-grained slush, and there were many new crevasses. The fixed ropes in the Icefall were also highly dangerous now, because the ice screws that anchored them in place had virtually melted out. They were so loose you could pull them out with your hand. The aluminum ladders spanning the crevasses were no longer long enough either; some had fallen into the depths as the rifts had widened. Furthermore, it was already past noon. Midday was the most dangerous time to pass through the Icefall, especially for a stumbling fool like me. I took the normal route and didn't bother about my own route that I'd searched out earlier. It wasn't the right time for principles.

I walked into the maze of ice. It had become an uncanny place. Water dripped from the icicles like in an old cellar, and all the time, I heard menacing cracks—like the sound of a frozen lake unthawing when the spring melt is coming. I knew that I ought to hurry down the glacier, but I couldn't. I was probably moving more slowly through the Icefall than anybody else had in history, and, to be honest, I no longer had even enough strength to be scared. I suffered from a deadly apathy, and I had to fight every impulse just to lie down and let sleep come.

I walked under a sixty-foot-long roof of ice formed by the glacier, and I got the uncanny feeling that it was not only waiting to collapse, but that it was preparing itself for a grandiose fall in which ten tons of ice would crush a miserable little creature like me. Death, I thought tiredly, would at least be kindly instantaneous. There were several good ways to die up here, and to die from exhaustion was supposed to be painless.

"Stop it!" I shouted at myself. "Keep moving!"

I came to a crevasse splitting the glacier, and a ladder that only just spanned it and reached to the other side. I balanced out onto the ladder—above a 150-foot-deep, cold, black void—and when I'd almost reached the other side, the ladder gave way underneath me. I threw myself forward, as if I was leaping for a lifeboat drifting away from me, and landed in a heap, safely, on the far bank. A little while later, I finally saw Base Camp in the distance.

It was a deserted little village. Many tents had disappeared while I'd been gone, and the camp looked more untidy than I remembered it. There was our stupa, our blessing altar. Some smoke was circling up from it, sacred juniper branches were smoldering, and the white smoke was carrying prayers up to the mountain gods. I thought of all the times on this expedition that, before I'd left Base Camp and started to climb, I had circled it three times, as the Sherpas always do, in reverence and for good luck. But now, as dusk settled over the Khumbu Valley on Saturday, the 25th of May, 1996, it was time for another ritual.

I walked up to our stupa, and I bowed deeply to it.

"I thank thee, Chomolungma, Everest. I thank thee for taking me up there, and I thank thee for letting me come back down."

Then something came creeping over me. A strange satisfaction spread like a faint light through my mangled body—it was the feeling of pure happiness. I took off my helmet and my crampons, threw them up into the air, and wheezed out a shout of joy. At that very moment, someone came running toward me, and then I saw who it was, and we embraced, and she exclaimed: "Göran! Göran!" and I tried to lift her—but I was too weak. I asked the Sherpas for a tub of hot water, and while I washed my body, the satellite phone started ringing, and it never stopped.

Epilogue

IN A FEW WEEKS, SOME 670 ARTICLES WERE WRITTEN about me, and still they kept coming. When I got to Kathmandu, I even was interviewed by magazines like *Newsweek* and *Time,* and I realized that I had done something that touched people. Some even thought that the Medal for a Great Achievement awarded by the Swedish newspaper *Svenska Dagbladet* should be given to me. The columnist Sune Sylvén compared climbing without supplemental oxygen to speedway racing without a helmet—a strange parallel since you can't go any faster driving without a helmet—but most of the articles that were written were very positive.

I had feared that the disaster of May 10 and 11 would rest like a dark shadow over my feat. The same day that I got back down to Base Camp, Bruce Harrod from the South African expedition died. I'd met him at Camp Four two days earlier, and then he seemed to be in good shape. Shortly before we met, he also had spoken with David Breashears.

Breashears told him: "Be careful. You know what happened two weeks ago. Remember that you're not an experienced climber!"

Bruce Harrod then climbed past Rob Hall's and Scott Fischer's dead bodies, but neither their fate nor Breashears's words taught him anything. He summitted all alone, and much too late, at 5:00 P.M. on May 25. And he died in an apparent fall while descending the Hillary Step. The sad thing is that others will continue to repeat his mistake. The tragedies on the mountain don't scare people off. Rather, they have had a fatal attraction, and in the spring of 1997, more climbers than ever before came to Mount Everest.

First, the Scottish mountain guide Mal Duff, who had built the route through the Icefall in 1996, was found dead — for no apparent reason — in his Base Camp tent. Then, two weeks later, on May 6 and 7, 1997, six climbers died in a snowstorm: three Russians, one German, and two Sherpas. Before that, in the postmonsoon season of 1996, on September 21, Scott Fischer's friend and protégé Lobsang Jangbu had died in an avalanche on Mount Everest. Lobsang always followed his mentor.

The cruel thing is that while all these additional tragedies happened on Everest, I received showers of congratulations. But more important to me, I now sometimes got the feeling that I had attained a significance that was almost existential to many people — and that I had ignited a yearning in them.

It took quite some time before I fully recovered.

The march down from Base Camp was hard. I was plagued by a painful cough, and for a long time, I had no feeling in my toes or fingers. I worried that something might have to be amputated.

I picked up my bicycle where I had left it, in the town of Jiri. Renata and I stayed in Nepal for a long time as I regained strength, and at the beginning of July, we set off for Sweden — on our bikes. It was another eventful journey, with absurd and unbelievable highlights.

Monsoon rains were pouring down, flooding the land and bringing out long leeches that stuck to me like suckers. The waters washed over the carcasses of dogs and water buffalo which lay scattered along the road. But I didn't mind the rain falling. I had been stressed to reach the summit of Mount Everest before the monsoon came, but now I was on my way home, and the deluge might as well keep us cool.

The heat in India gave me a rash, and when the rain stopped, the rash turned into open wounds, attracting flies. To make myself happy — and to help a poor creature — I bought a monkey, a baboon, tied to an iron pole. He ran around the pole like a maniac, as if he thought he would get somewhere if only he ran fast enough. I gave 500 rupees to the salesman who was standing at the roadside in front of some tiny cages with shrieking parrots. The monkey looked bewildered, as if he had never known that there were paths to follow other than circles. Then he shrieked in triumph and disappeared up a tree. I thrived on the memory of that scene for a long time. I thought about it while we went through Delhi, past Murthal and Ambala, toward Pakistan and the Karakorum Highway, and down to the Indus Valley.

In Pakistan the road cut through the mountains, and sometimes we passed under rocks hanging above us. "This is Himalaya's birthplace," a sign stated. We were in the area where the continents collided some fifty-five million years ago, pushing against each other and forcing up this giant mountain range. The tallest mountain in the world was born here. Below us lay the river Indus. Tributary brooks with emerald green water fed into the gray sludge of the river. It could have been a wonderful day. . . . But stones were flying through the air. Deadly boulders. Young boys sitting on the rocks hovering over the road tried to drop big stones on us. I could never figure out why.

One day we were rolling down a long slope. I had taken the lead with my long bike trailer. Renata was behind me. Along the road, we saw goats and shepherds with long crooks, and I thought they used the crooks for herding their sheep. But when we swished by, one of the guys raised his crook. I saw a scary-looking hook at the end of it, and that idiot tried to catch Renata with it. I jammed the brakes and jumped off my bike. But the shepherds fled, all of them dressed in the same damned pajamas, and when I reached a cornfield, I gave up.

But I had gotten his crook. I broke it in two and kept it handy on the bike. Every time we entered a village and people picked up stones, I waved the crook and laughed like a maniac: *Ha, ha, ha!* I don't know if the people had seen any low-budget horror movies, but I tried to sound like one of those crazy killers who finds pleasure in being evil, and it helped. People didn't dare throw stones — they just stared. "Who's that maniac?" they seemed to think. "Who's the lunatic?"

Sometimes I wondered myself. I'm peaceful by nature. But cyclists more peaceable than I have been driven to manufacture old-fashioned maces and nail guns to defend themselves on the Karakorum Highway. As of yet, I hadn't gone *that* far. I was just tired of having to wear my climbing helmet on the bike in order to keep my head from getting smashed.

The Karakorum Highway, which took twenty years to build, is a two-lane asphalt road from Islamabad in Pakistan to Kashgar in China; it runs through the world's tallest mountain ranges. It's sometimes called the Eighth Wonder of the World. Nowadays, many Westerners bike here, so you would have thought that the hostile feelings against us had subsided, but people who smiled and called, "Allah be with you!" could attack us a few seconds later.

One day, when I had the crook on my bike, I saw a boy in a white shalwar. He had a big stone in his hand and he was aiming it at Renata's back. I shouted and the boy fled over the yellow grass. I ran after him with the crook in my hand, up to a small stone house with a rusty iron gate that creaked when the boy tore it open. I was right behind him as he ran inside, through a simple kitchen and out into a garden with one solitary tree. It was an atrium, a small garden in the middle of the house. In the corner, there were some farming implements, and hens were clucking all around us.

Now I had him. I kicked him and he fell to the ground, and not until then did it occur to me what a weird situation this was. "How did I end up here?" I thought. Right then, two giant women came out through the door, shouting in fury and flailing their arms like windmills. I sensed their angry faces under their dark veils. One picked up a large stone and threw it at my back.

"Ouch!" I cried and looked at her angrily. It was as if neither one of us understood what was going on—a moment of madness. My back hurt, and the giant bodies of the women seemed to swell in the heat, and suddenly all my chivalry was gone and I attacked. I kicked one of the women—a 300-pound matron—as hard as I could. At that, the other woman went into a side room and came back with something that looked like an axe. I remained where I was, ready for anything. Then a whole crowd appeared, and they all looked like they were engaged in a holy war against Göran Kropp. So I rushed for my bike, narrowly escaping the axe handle that came flying over my shoulder.

The sun was still high in the sky. As I ran over the field, I looked out over the road and the valley. I realized that before I could mount my bike and work up some speed, the whole gang would be on me, so I stopped and picked up some stones and threw them at my pursuers to slow them down. "What a circus!" I thought. "What madness!"

In a few days, Renata and I were planning to fly to Friedrichshafen to attend an outdoor sports fair with one of my sponsors, and here I was, pedaling away on my bike, armed with stones and an iron crook. The landscape became ever more barren and desert-like. Somewhere around here was Ultar Peak, one of the tallest unscaled mountains in the world at that time. What a tempting challenge. Still, I mostly wanted clean sheets and good food. I wanted peace and quiet.

But the stones kept flying at us. The road went uphill and downhill until we finally reached a whitewashed hotel with a large terrace down by the river. A beautiful place. We had planned to cover more road that day, but we were exhausted and angry, so we parked our bikes for the night and entered a whitewashed lobby with black leather easy chairs. A tall man in a light-colored uniform greeted us, but at that moment our anger erupted.

"What's wrong with us?" Renata shouted.

"Nothing!" the man behind the reception desk answered, bewildered.

"But why does everyone want to kill us?!"

"Kill you?" the man repeated, sounding shocked.

Soon, the hotel manager came, and he solemnly vowed to file a report about the assaults. We calmed down and went out on the terrace and had Cokes by the river in the refreshing afternoon air. There was a light breeze. On the hillsides, there were solitary silver firs and Himalayan pines, and far away, I could see snow-covered peaks. I wiggled my toes and fingers. On the march out from Base Camp, I thought they had gotten frostbitten. Now they were fine, and the dry cough I had had on the mountain was long since gone. "Life isn't too bad after all," I thought and looked out over the Indus. "But I've had enough of madness and tragedies now. It's been a long journey."

And it wasn't over yet. Iran was closed to us. Women weren't allowed to bicycle there. And unfortunately, we couldn't get a Russian visa, either. After a lot of hassle, I relented on another of my principles. We took the train, second class, from Alma-Ata in Kazakhstan to Moscow. It would have been easy to bike that distance, but we didn't dare do it without a visa. From Moscow to St.

Petersburg, we decided to bicycle without one, but we were very nervous. I had a computer and a phone with me, and this was at a time when two Swedes had recently been arrested in Russia and accused on flimsy evidence of espionage.

While we were still in Russia, we saw a Saab with a Swedish license plate on the road, and of course we waved happily to it. The car stopped, and out stepped the Eastern European journalist Staffan Skott.

"Is it you, you crazy bastard?" he said to me.

We told him we had neither money nor visa—we hadn't dared change currency—so Staffan loaned us some, for which I am very grateful.

In St. Petersburg, we bought Russian champagne. We opened the bottle in our tent when we reached Finnish Karelia, and then we took the ferry across the Baltic to Sweden. On October 16, 1997 — one year to the day after I had left the city—I kissed the ground beside the Stockholm harbor.

Roger Blomqvist from Informedia met us at the harbor. He had been handling my press contacts, and joked about getting a brass band and a parade to meet me.

"Stop!" I told him. "Enough's enough."

But when I cycled along Hornsgatan Street, cars began honking. People cheered, and at the far end of the little street Yttersta Tvärgränd, where I'd started my journey, a crowd of journalists was waiting.

I got even more attention in my hometown of Jönköping. I also received strict orders not to come home before October 22 — the town needed time to organize.

When I approached Jönköping, a soft rain was falling. I looked out over Lake Vättern and began thinking about my wild teenage years, the singer Eva Dahlgren and all that—when suddenly I heard sirens. It was my police escort. The police took me to the town's central park where, even though it was a workday and was raining, 300 people had gathered. I received lots of gifts and speeches of thanks, but what I remember best was drinking a beer out of a plastic bag.

I was given this gift by a local wino. No older than thirty-five, he wore a threadbare denim jacket and a bandanna around his neck, and had a pinch of snuff tucked under his upper lip.

"I don't know what to give you," he said, hesitating a little. "But you deserve this," he said, handing me the plastic bag filled with beer.

I could tell by the look in his eyes that this was quite a big sacrifice for him, so I drank it gratefully. Then I walked home, lit a candle, drew a hot bath, and had a glass of champagne.

The year that followed was strangely hectic. I gave talks like never before, and I was always asked the question: "Why? Why did you do it?"

I don't know if I have managed to give some kind of answer to that question in this book, but I have, I think, tried my best to do so. We are all different, and some of us have wilder dreams than others. That's the way I see it, and I don't know why my dreams look the way they do. Do you?

As I'm writing this, an American space probe has just landed on Mars. The picture that was transmitted all over the world showed a hilly landscape. A picture like that makes me shiver. I get excited. No matter how long you walk in that landscape, you won't find a single hotel or a gas station. But what would you see all around you on Mars? The unknown. And what would you think about in a desolate place like that? You would explore! If a country, an international organization, or a multinational company asked for volunteers to go on a journey to an unknown planet, I'd be the first one to put up my hand.

"I want to go!" I would shout like a little kid.

I envy the people of tomorrow and those of yore. Nowadays, there are no blank spots on the map, no new places on the globe to discover, and God knows how long it will take before a new generation of discoverers sets out on journeys through space. I wish I could be one of them.

In the spring and early summer of 1997, I climbed with Renata and a few others on the mountain Shisha Pangma (26,397 feet) in Tibet. This time, the show belonged to Renata. She was surprisingly strong, and she became the first Swedish woman to reach 8,000 meters without supplemental oxygen. But apart from that, I have turned my gaze away from the tallest peaks.

I am seeking other types of challenges now. Reinhold Messner has scaled all fourteen 8,000-meter peaks in the world without using supplemental oxygen. The sad thing is, you can tell. His personality has gotten strange, and the thin air has probably damaged his brain. People say that he is like an old boxer who's taken too many punches. I don't want to become like that, so now I am focused on Antarctica — the closest thing to another planet that there is on this earth.

The South Pole is what I dream about nowadays.

One of the astronauts who went to the moon said that Antarctica was the most eye-catching place on the globe. It reflects the light of the sun like a giant white lantern at the bottom of the globe. The continent of Antarctica is the size of India and China combined, and even though ninety-eight percent is covered with ice, it is a diversified world. In its interior, you find the South Pole, where Earth's axis hits.

In Antarctica, the inland ice has created giant domes and unfathomably deep crevasses next to rocky mountain peaks—

called nunataks—that rise like spears from the glacier. In the Ellsworth Mountains, there's the Vinson Massif, which reaches an altitude of 16,067 feet, and not far away, there are volcanoes that have thrown burning lava over vast areas. There are even a few freshwater lakes and ice-free valleys on the continent, covered with stones polished by the wind, some sand dunes, too, and salt crusts. And there are areas where there is hardly ever any rain or snow, a place in Antarctica without precipitation.

Imagine walking—or skiing—alone across this vast continent. I do.

Antarctica has no indigenous human population, but there are abandoned harbor buildings once used for seal-hunting and whaling, and a number of scientific stations. In spite of the barren landscape and arid ground—only mosses and lichen grow here—there is a spectacular diversity of fauna.

There are metropolises in Antarctica, population centers where close to a million penguins gather, croaking loudly. Forty-five different species of birds live on the continent: albatrosses, fulmars, cormorants, gulls, snow-white petrels; and in the ocean waters swim swarms of transparent shrimp called krill, and whales, dolphins, porpoises, and various species of seal, including sea elephants and sea leopards.

Antarctica was the last continent on Earth to be discovered. The British explorer Robert Scott had decided he would become the first human being to reach the South Pole. When he got there in January of 1912, his expedition was exhausted, but it was a moment of triumph; they were the first people at the Pole—or so they thought, until they saw something fluttering nearby: a Norwegian flag. Roald Amundsen, who had hurried across the continent with four sleds, five men, and fifty-two dogs, had beaten him to the Pole by a month. Robert Scott and his three companions starved to death on their return journey.

Eighty-four years later—while I was biking across Europe

and Asia toward Mount Everest—the British and Norwegians were competing in Antarctica again. Norwegian explorer and skier Børge Oulsand's goal was to be the first to cross the continent alone. As I chose to do on Mount Everest, Ousland wouldn't let anyone else help him. He skied with climbing skins while dragging a 375-pound sledge holding all his supplies. He got up at 5:50 A.M. each day, and occasionally used a sail to speed up his journey across the ice. He played Jimi Hendrix on his Walkman.

But somewhere behind him in the snowy landscape, another man traveled alone. It was the Brit Roger Mear, and he was vying for the same record. Both men claimed that it was a coincidence that they tried to cross Antarctica at the same time. Ousland even said that he didn't know anything about Mear's plans until he booked his flight on the only airline flying to Antarctica—and saw Mear's name on the passenger list. And there were others chasing them, too, including Marek Kaminiski, who had recently crossed the North Pole alone.

The first to drop out of the race was Mear. He gave up after forty-one days. The next one was Ousland, who got an inflammation in a wound in his leg, caused by severe frostbite, when he was only a couple of days short of the South Pole. Soon thereafter, Kaminiski gave up, too.

But, as opposed to the others, Ousland didn't really give up. Thirteen months later, he was back in Antarctica—and on January 18, 1997, he became the first human to cross the ice- and snow-covered continent alone.

So I won't be the first doing that. But my idea is to travel single-handedly all the way from Sweden to the South Pole. I will sail alone to Antarctica, anchor my boat on the coast—if I can; much of the Antarctic coastline is hundred-foot-high ice cliffs—ski to the South Pole, then sail home again.

The problem is that I have never sailed before. The waves and seas in "the roaring forties" north of the continent are horrible, plus there are cyclones, blizzards, hurricanes, and katabatic winds—which are monstrously strong wind gusts. The average wind speed on Antarctica is thirty-four miles per hour, and in the ocean there are additional obstacles: icebergs and drifting pack ice.

I know that I will have to prepare meticulously for the next five or six years. Roger Nilsson, the Whitbread sailor, mentioned a colleague from Uruguay who sailed to Antarctica. I will talk to him. And I will read every single word written on the subject. Adventurers have to study, too.

First and foremost, I will learn to sail. It may sound like madness that I, who have never sailed before, intend to undertake the most difficult sailing adventure, perhaps, that there is. But I like to jump headfirst into new projects. According to the sailor Thomas Gross, you should start with a small boat, like a Laser, because then you can really feel the wind. You get to know its gusts and whims. Then I'm going to spend all my time at sea.

People have sailed to Antarctica, and people have made it alone from the coast of the continent to the South Pole, but no one has done both. Perhaps I, too, will discover that it's impossible, but I will do everything I can to investigate the possibility of this adventure, and sometime around 2004, I will sail away from Sweden, heading south.

One obvious problem is the contrast between sailing and skiing. When I reach Antarctica after eight months or so on the ocean, my muscles will be weak from lack of exercise. Will I have enough physical power to ski 750 miles to the South Pole?

Børge Ousland began his Antarctic crossing with a 375-pound load of food and supplies. I can probably get by with 330 pounds. After my Everest expedition, I'm a specialist at packing light. The weight of the food I will need to carry will be the difficult part. I'll probably need over three pounds of food per day, and since the trip to the Pole and back takes around ninety days—or less, hopefully—my food supply will weigh well over 200 pounds when I start. But I know already, from personal experience, that to pull is easier than to carry! Halfway across, I will leave a cache containing the food that I need for my return journey.

The polar night lasts for six months, and in July, the coldest time of the year, temperatures as low as minus 129 degrees Fahrenheit have been recorded. I will make my ski journey to the Pole in January, the warmest month, but even then, the average temperature in the heart of the continent is minus 30 degrees. Gales blow and there are no living beings in sight, not until you reach the research station at the South Pole. In spite of all these adversities, I can't wait to start on my way.

I imagine how I will anchor my boat not far from an iceberg that looks like a giant hand. Perhaps a humpback whale splashes nearby, and out on the ice, two penguins chatter. I can see it now: An albatross hovers in midair above me, and a cloud, white as chalk, is lit up by the purity of the snow below.

On the shore, covered by algae and smooth stones, a Weddell seal sleeps, and in the blue, almost-violet sky hangs a pale moon. I look around, from left to right, and on the horizon, I can see a range of jagged mountains. A fulmar alights on the ground. A creature looking like a man dressed in tails walks along in the distance.

This is my next dream. I set out into the great white solitude.

The Kropp Ultimate Mountain List

		PEAK	COUNTRY	HT. IN FT.
+	1.	Mount Everest	Nepal / Tibet	29,028
+	2.	K2	Pakistan / Tibet	28,251
	3.	Kangchenjunga	Nepal / India	28,169
+	4.	Cho Oyu	Nepal / Tibet	26,906
+	5.	Broad Peak	Pakistan / India	26,401
+	6.	Peak Pobeda	Kyrgyzstan	24,406
+	7.	Muztagh Tower	Pakistan / Tibet	23,862
+	8.	Pik Lenin	Kyrgyzstan / Tajikistan	23,406
	9.	Aconcagua	Argentina	22,834
+	10.	Illampu	Bolivia	21,276
+	11.	Illimani	Bolivia	20,741
	12.	Mount McKinley	Alaska, USA	20,320
+	13.	Huyana Potosi	Bolivia	19,997
+	14.	Cotopaxi	Ecuador	19,347
+	15.	Kilimanjaro	Tanzania	19,340
	16.	Elbrus	Russia	18,510
+	17.	Illiniza Sur	Ecuador	17,277
+	18.	Mont Blanc	France / Italy	15,771
	19.	Mount Kinabalu	Borneo	13,455
	20.	Gunnbjorn Fjeld	Greenland	12,139
+	21.	Kebnekaise	Sweden	6,926
+	22.	Kaga Tondo	Mali	3,789

+   PEAK SCALED BY GÖRAN KROPP

Packing List

Sweden to Everest Solo Expedition 1995/96

STOVE AND FOOD

ITEM	QUANTITY	WT. IN OZ.
Primus stove with cookset	1	42
Victorinox knife	1	6.0
Food thermos	1	21
Thermos bag	1	5.6
Water bag, one gallon	1	0.9
Primus gas canister, small	6	71
Primus gas canister, large	10	212
Freeze-dried main courses	32	158
Freeze-dried soups	112	257
Dextrose drinks	56	128
Chocolate drinks	56	99
Crackers, packages	56 (8)	296
Chocolate bars	28	64
Candy, packages	55	62
Dextrose tablets, packages	7 (2)	11.6
PowerBars	11 (2)	39
Salt/pepper	1	2.5
Wholemeal gruel, package	1	35

TOTAL WEIGHT, STOVE AND FOOD: **94 LBS., 7 OZ.**

CLIMBING GEAR

ITEM	QUANTITY	WT. IN OZ.
Helmet, Petzl Ecrin	1	15
Ice axes, Charlet Moser, Pulsar Compact	2	45
Crampons, Charlet Moser, Black Ice	1 pair	34
Rope, Rivory Joanny Virus	165 ft.	134
Harness, Gourou XL	1	17
Ice screws	3	9.0
Dead man	1	6.5
Locking carabiner/HMS	2/1	3.9/3.0
Carabiners	4	7.8
Chocks, sizes 2, 4, 6, 8, 10	5	7.4
Grigri belay device	1	7.9
Sewn runners, 24 in.	3	6.3
Accessory cord, 5 mm	16 ft.	1.8
Climbing boots, One Sport Everest	1 pair	120
Telescoping poles, Salewa	1 pair	22

TOTAL WEIGHT, CLIMBING GEAR: **27 LBS., 9 OZ.**

BIKING EQUIPMENT

ITEM	QUANTITY	WT. IN OZ.
Bicycle, Crescent Ultima	1	
Bicycle trailer, Packtrack	1	
Bicycle bags, Quorum	4	1,103
Bicycle meter, Avocet	1	
Lights	3 (2)	
Cable locks	2	22
Tires	2	55
Tubes	3	20
Chain	2 (1)	13
Spokes, front/back	10/20	7
Brake shoes	4	3.2
Spare back wheel	(1)	49
Tube repair kit	2	1.8
Cycle pump	1	6.7
Tools: multi-purpose tool, chain riveting tool, monkey wrench, spoke wrench, hexagonal wrench, wrench size 10/11, pair of pliers, tire remover	1 of each	39
Cycling pants, Crescent	3	21
Cycling gloves, Hestra	1	1.8
Cycling shoes, Salomon	1	38

TOTAL WEIGHT, BIKING EQUIPMENT: 86 LBS., 4 OZ.

TENT, CLOTHING, ETC.

ITEM	QUANTITY	WT. IN OZ.
Tent, Haglöfs	1	42
Tent, Wild Country	(1)	120
Backpack, Haglöfs Climber, 4,900 cu. in.	1	85
Small backpack, Haglöfs, 900 cu. in.	7	
Kit bag, Haglöfs, 7,300 cu. in.	1	14
Sleeping bag, Haglöfs	1	42
Sleeping pad, Ridge Rest	1 (1)	14
Shell clothing, Haglöfs Guide	1	67
Fleece sweater and pants, Haglöfs	1	34
Pile Salopettes, Javlin	1	42
Underwear set, Termo	1	18
Underwear set, Termo light	2	28
Underwear set, Craft	1	10
Shorts, Craft	1	2.5
Balaclava, Sätila	1	6.7
Peaked cap, Sätila	1	2.6
The Kropp glove, Hestra	1	7.8
Woolen mitten/glove, Hestra	1 each	6.7/3.9
Socks, gray, Bola	2	4.2
Socks, blue, Bola	1	2.5
Socks, Hike, Bola	3	7.4
Thick socks, Bola	1	6.3

TOTAL WEIGHT, TENT, CLOTHING, ETC.:   35 LBS., 14 OZ.

MISCELLANEOUS

ITEM	QUANTITY	WT. IN OZ.
Cell phone with accessories	1	7.2
Camera, Fuji	1	11
*IBM Thinkpad 701 CS	1	121
*System camera, Nikon FE2	(1)	29
*Lenses, 20 mm and 70–210 mm	1 each	9.5/23
*Camcorder	1	33
Film, Fuji Velvia	20	21
Video film, Fuji E5-90	5	11
Headlamp, Petzl Arctic	(1)	6.2
Satellite phone with accessories, Glocom	1	295
Walkman and tapes	1/5	12/12
Battery charger, Energizer	1	15
Rechargeable batteries, Energizer	6	4.2
Toiletries/medication	1 set each	25
Visa card	1	.2
Passport	1	1.1
*Maps	3	9.0
Notepad and pen	1	4.9

TOTAL WEIGHT, MISCELLANEOUS: 40 LBS., 10 OZ.

TOTAL WEIGHT, EXPEDITION: 284 LBS., 12 OZ.

TOTAL WEIGHT DURING APPROACH: 161 LBS.

NOTE: SOME WEIGHTS ARE ESTIMATED (MEDICATION, FOR EXAMPLE).

( ) BOUGHT IN NEPAL / SENT DOWN

* ONLY ON THE BICYCLE

Distance List

DATE	PLACE	MILES
	Yttre Tvärgränd	0
10/16	Hölö Church	38.0
10/17	Norrköping	74.8
10/18	Kisa	65.3
10/19	Vetlanda	63.2
10/20	Tofta	40.7
10/21	Osby	47.2
10/22	Klinta	55.3
10/23	Trelleborg	45.7
TOTAL SWEDEN		**430.2**
TOTAL INCLUDING SWEDEN		**430.2**
10/24	Malchin	50.5
10/25	Gransee	71.8
10/26	Zossen	62.6
10/27	Bluno	71.5
10/28	Ebersbach	54.4
TOTAL GERMANY		**310.8**
TOTAL INCLUDING GERMANY		**741.0**
10/29	Ceska Lipa	35.7
10/30	Hradec Kralove	78.8
10/31	Brezhova	59.1
11/1	Zidlochovice	50.1
TOTAL CZECH REPUBLIC		**223.7**
TOTAL INCLUDING CZECH REPUBLIC		**964.7**
11/2	Bratislava	77.2
TOTAL SLOVAKIA		**77.2**
TOTAL INCLUDING SLOVAKIA		**1,041.9**
11/3	Komarom	64.9
11/4	Dorog	33.2
11/5	Dabas	57.2
11/6	Kiskunfelegyhaza	60.2
11/7	Apatfalva	50.1
TOTAL HUNGARY		**265.6**
TOTAL INCLUDING HUNGARY		**1,307.5**

DATE	PLACE	MILES
11/8	Arad	57.7
11/9	Chizatan	61.6
11/10	Motel Silvia	51.2
11/11	Turnu Severin	62.5
TOTAL RUMANIA		**233.0**
TOTAL INCLUDING RUMANIA		**1,540.5**
11/12	Vidin	68.6
11/13	Smoljanovci	47.0
11/14	Vraca	48.0
11/15	Cureski prohod	44.4
11/16	Karlovo	68.9
11/17	Plovdiv	41.1
11/18	Harmanli	72.5
TOTAL BULGARIA		**390.5**
TOTAL INCLUDING BULGARIA		**1,931.0**
11/19	Havsa	58.8
11/20	Luleburgaz	32.2
11/21	Silvri	58.3
11/22	Istanbul	43.5
11/23	Hereke	53.5
11/24	Izmit	27.2
11/25	Duzce	63.4
11/26	Bolu	31.8
11/27	Gerede	48.6
11/28	Kursunlu	54.3
11/29	Balkyisi	67.4
11/30	Saraycik	47.0
12/1	Amasya	54.2
12/2	Erbaa	49.7
12/3	Resadiye	55.6
12/4	Koyulhisar	32.7
12/5	Cobanli	52.4
12/6	Erzincan	57.3
12/7	Altunkent	47.4
12/8	Askale	42.1
12/9	Erzurum	34.1
12/10	Erzurum	0
12/11	Horasan	65.7
12/12	Agri	53.5
12/13	Dogubayazit	60.4
TOTAL TURKEY		**1,191.1**
TOTAL INCLUDING TURKEY		**3,122.1**

DATE	PLACE	MILES
12/14	Marganlar	62.3
12/15	Marand	93.4
12/16	Tabriz	54.8
12/17	Qarahchman	62.0
12/18	Mianeh (Tehran)	21.4
12/19	Tehran	0
12/20	a field	68.6
12/21	a factory	69.0
12/22	Qazvin	86.3
12/23	Karaj	66.9
12/24	Tehran	29.8
12/25	Tehran	0
12/26	the desert	42.1
12/27	Qom	64.3
12/28	Kashan	59.8
12/29	Kashan	0
12/30	Natanz	35.3
12/31	Ardestan	46.9
1/1	Ardakan	55.5
1/2	Mehriz	81.0
1/3	Anar	65.6
1/4	Ahmad Abad	85.3
1/5	Kerman	77.5
1/6	Mahan	46.3
1/7	Baravat	106.6
1/8	Kahurak	97.1
1/9	Zahedan	67.8
1/10	Mirjaveh	55.4
TOTAL IRAN		**1,601.0**
TOTAL INCLUDING IRAN		**4,723.1**
1/11	the desert, Nok Kundi	72.5
1/12	the desert, Nok Kundi	60.4
1/13	Yakmach	63.3
1/14	Karadok	44.6
1/15	a field, Nushki	71.3
1/16	Nushki	47.4
1/17	Dalbandi	3.7
1/18	Quetta	85.1
1/19	Quetta	0
1/20	Quetta	0
1/21	Murgha Mehterzai	57.9
1/22	Quila Saifullah	58.2
1/23	Loralai	55.4

DATE	PLACE	MILES
1/24	Mekhtar	59.4
1/25	Rakhni	63.9
1/26	Sakhi Sarwar	42.7
1/27	Multan	77.1
1/28	the desert	47.8
1/29	Pakpattan	68.2
1/30	Suleimanki	68.2
1/31	Qazur	66.0
2/1	Lahore	63.9
2/2	Lahore	0
TOTAL PAKISTAN		**1,177.0**
TOTAL INCLUDING PAKISTAN		**5,900.1**
2/3	Amritsar	62.3
2/4	Ludhiana	65.4
2/5	Ambala	65.3
2/6	Karnal	61.6
2/7	Delhi	90.7
2/8	Delhi	8.4
2/9	Delhi	0
2/10	Babugarh	57.3
2/11	Moradabad	66.0
2/12	Faridpur	73.8
2/13	Maigalganj	59.7
2/14	Itaunia	69.4
2/15	Bara Banki	50.5
2/16	Ayodhya	64.2
2/17	Khalilabad	64.4
2/18	Nutwana	55.2
TOTAL INDIA		**914.2**
TOTAL INCLUDING INDIA		**6,814.3**
2/19	Baihwala	46.7
2/20	Chitawan	58.9
2/21	Maleku	48.1
2/22	Kathmandu	50.3
	Dhuleki	37.6
	Charikot	54.0
	Jiri	45.2
TOTAL NEPAL		**340.8**
TOTAL INCLUDING NEPAL		**7,155.1**

Special Summiteer List

As of October 1, 1997, 932 people had reached the top of Everest.
The following list reflects unique achievements among summiteers, or
summits by characters in the book.

#	NAME	NATION	DATE
1	Edmund Hillary	New Zealand	5/29/53
2	Tenzing Norgay Sherpa	India	
	South Col to Southeast Ridge.		
7	Wang Fu-chou	China	5/25/60
8	Gonpa	China	
9	Chu Ying-hua	China	
	North Col to North Ridge.		
	First ascent from Tibetan side; claim disputed.		
14	Willi Unsoeld	U.S.	5/22/63
15	Tom Hornbein	U.S.	
	West Ridge from Cwm up;		
	Southeast Ridge to South Col down.		
	First ascent of West Ridge; first traverse of Everest.		
17	Nawang Gombu Sherpa	India	5/20/65
	South Col to Southeast Ridge.		
	His 2nd ascent. First person to climb Everest twice.		
37	Yasuo Kato	Japan	10/26/73
38	Hisashi Ishiguro	Japan	
	South Col to Southeast Ridge.		
	First autumn ascent.		
39	Junko Tabei	Japan	5/16/75
	South Col to Southeast Ridge.		
	First woman to summit. First all-woman expedition.		
50	Dougal Haston	U.K.	9/24/75
51	Doug Scott	U.K.	
52	Peter Boardman	U.K.	9/26/75
53	Pertempa Sherpa	Nepal	
	Southwest Face.		
	First ascent of Southwest Face.		
64	Reinhold Messner	Italy	5/8/78
65	Peter Habeler	Austria	
	South Col to Southeast Ridge.		
	First to summit without use of bottled oxygen.		
68	Franz Oppurg	Austria	5/14/78
	First to reach summit solo from last camp.		
85	Jernej Zaplotnik	Yugoslavia	5/13/79
86	Andrej Stremfelj	Yugoslavia	
	West Ridge from South (from Lho La).		
	First people to reach summit via entire West Ridge.		
89	Ang Phu Sherpa	Nepal	5/15/79
	His 2nd ascent. First person to climb Everest via two routes. Died in fall during descent.		
103	Leszek Cichy	Poland	2/17/80

#	NAME	NATION	DATE
104	Krzysztof Wielicki	Poland	
	South Col to Southeast Ridge.		
	First winter ascent of any 8,000-meter peak.		
105	Yasuo Kato	Japan	5/3/80
	North Ridge. His 2nd ascent.		
	First person to climb north and south sides.		
	First non-Sherpa to climb twice.		
106	Takashi Ozaki	Japan	5/10/80
	North Face.		
	First ascent of North Face.		
107	Tsuneo Shigehiro	Japan	
110	Andrzej Czok	Poland	5/19/80
	South Pillar to South Summit.		
	First ascent of South Pillar.		
111	Jersy Kukuczka	Poland	
112	Reinhold Messner	Italy	8/20/80
	(solo)		
	North Col to North Ridge to North Face.		
	His 2nd ascent.		
	First completely solo ascent. Used no bottled oxygen.		
	First person to summit twice without bottled oxygen.		
	First summer ascent.		
130	Sungdare Sherpa	Nepal	10/5/82
	South Col to Southeast Ridge.		
	His 3rd ascent. First person to climb three times.		
135	Yasuo Kato	Japan	12/27/82
	South Col to Southeast Ridge.		
	First person to climb in three different seasons.		
	His 3rd ascent. Died during descent; cause unknown.		
140	Ang Rita Sherpa	Nepal	5/7/83
	South Col to Southeast Ridge.		
	Used no bottled oxygen.		
144	Louis Reichardt	U.S.	10/8/83
145	Carlos Buhler	U.S.	
146	Kim Momb	U.S.	
147	Dan Reid	U.S.	10/9/83
148	George Lowe	U.S.	
149	Jay Cassell	U.S.	
	First ascent of East Face; to Southeast Ridge.		
174	Ang Rita Sherpa	Nepal	10/15/84
	South Pillar to Southeast Ridge up; Southeast Ridge to		
	South Col down. His 2nd ascent. Used no bottled oxygen.		
176	Chris Bonington	U.K.	4/21/85
177	Odd Eliassen	Norway	
178	Björn Myrer-Lund	Norway	
179	Pertemba Sherpa	Nepal	
	His 3rd ascent.		
180	Ang Lhakpa Sherpa	Nepal	
181	Dawa Norbu Sherpa	Nepal	
182	Arne Naess	Norway	4/29/85
183	Stein Aasheim	Norway	
184	Ralph Hoibakk	Norway	
185	Havard Nesheim	Norway	

#	NAME	NATION	DATE
186	Sungdare Sherpa	Nepal	
	First person to climb four times.		
	His 4th ascent.		
187	Ang Rita Sherpa	Nepal	
	His 3rd ascent. Used no bottled oxygen.		
190	Richard Bass	U.S.	4/30/85
	At 55, oldest summiteer to date.		
	South Col to Southeast Ridge.		
208	Erhard Loretan	Switzerland	8/30/86
209	Jean Troillet	Switzerland	
	North Face in swift, alpine-style climb.		
	Neither used bottled oxygen.		
211	Ang Rita Sherpa	Nepal	12/22/87
	South Col to Southeast Ridge.		
	His 4th ascent. Used no bottled oxygen.		
	First winter ascent without supplemental oxygen.		
231	Jean-Marc Boivin	France	9/26/88
	South Col to Southeast Ridge.		
	Paraglided from summit to Camp Two at 21,000 feet.		
245	Marc Batard	France	9/26/88
	South Col to Southeast Ridge.		
	Fastest ascent; climbed alone from Base Camp to top in 22.5 hours.		
	(Not truly solo; there were others on the same route at the same time.)		
	Used no bottled oxygen.		
258	Ang Rita Sherpa	Nepal	10/14/88
	South Col to Southeast Ridge.		
	His 5th ascent. Used no bottled oxygen.		
286	Ang Rita Sherpa	Nepal	4/23/90
	South Col to Southeast Ridge.		
	First person to climb six times. No bottled oxygen.		
319	Peter Hillary	New Zealand	5/10/90
	South Col to Southeast Ridge.		
	First son of any summiteer to summit.		
324	Mikael Reuterswärd	Sweden	5/11/90
325	Oskar Kihlborg	Sweden	
326	Tim McCartney-Snape	Australia	5/11/90
	South Col to Southeast Ridge.		
	First person to go on foot from sea level to summit.		
	His 2nd ascent. Used no bottled oxygen.		
335	Jean Noel Roche	France	10/7/90
336	Bertrand Roche	France	
	South Col to Southeast Ridge. First father and son ascent.		
	B. Roche, age 17, youngest non-Nepalese to summit.		
355	Andrej Stremfelj	Yugoslavia	10/7/90
356	Marija Stremfelj	Yugoslavia	
	South Col to Southeast Ridge.		
	His 2nd ascent. First married couple to summit together.		
379	Lars Cronlund	Sweden	5/20/91
	North Face via the Japanese and Horbein Couloirs.		

SPECIAL SUMMITEER LIST

#	NAME	NATION	DATE
451	Ang Rita Sherpa	Nepal	5/15/92
	South Col to Southeast Ridge.		
	His 7th ascent. Used no bottled oxygen.		
456	Alberto Inurrategi	Spain	9/25/92
	Felix Inurrategi	Spain	
	South Col to Southeast Ridge.		
	First brothers to summit together. They used no bottled oxygen.		
522	Santosh Yadav	India	5/10/93
	South Col to Southeast Ridge.		
	First woman to climb twice.		
549	Veikka Gustafsson	Finland	5/10/93
	South Col to Southeast Ridge.		
568	Ang Rita Sherpa	Nepal	5/16/93
	South Col to Southeast Ridge.		
	His 8th ascent. Used no bottled oxygen.		
591	Ramon Blanco	Spain	10/7/93
	South Col to Southeast Ridge.		
	Aged 60, oldest summiteer so far.		
606	Lhakpa Nuru Sherpa	Nepal	10/9/93
	North Col to North Face.		
	His 4th ascent. First person to climb by 3 different routes.		
667	Kiyoshi Furuno	Japan	5/11/95
668	Shigeki Imoto	Japan	
669	Dawa Tshering Sherpa	Nepal	
	His 2nd ascent.		
670	Pasang Kami Sherpa	Nepal	
	His 2nd ascent.		
671	Lhakpa Nuru Sherpa	Nepal	
	His 6th ascent.		
	Along with no. 672, first person to climb by 4 different routes.		
672	Nima Dorje Sherpa	Nepal	
	First ascent of Northeast Ridge.		
	His 5th ascent.		
680	Ang Rita Sherpa	Nepal	5/13/95
	North Col to North Ridge.		
	His 9th ascent. Used no bottled oxygen.		
690	Michael Jörgensen	Denmark	5/23/95
	North Col to North Ridge.		
697	Alison Hargreaves	U.K.	5/13/95
	North Col to North Ridge. Used no bottled oxygen.		
	First woman to summit on an unsupported climb.		
711	Wongchu Sherpa	Nepal	5/14/95
	North Col to North Ridge.		
728	Babu Tshering Sherpa	Nepal	5/26/95
	North Col to North Ridge. His 5th ascent.		
	First person to make two ascents in the same season.		
749	Anatoli Boukreev	Kazakhstan	5/10/96
	His 3rd ascent.		
750	Neal Beidleman	U.S.	
751	Martin Adams	U.S.	
752	Klev Schoening	U.S.	
753	Charlotte Fox	U.S.	

#	NAME	NATION	DATE
754	Tim Madsen	U.S.	
755	Sandy Hill Pittman	U.S.	
756	Scott Fischer	U.S.	

His 2nd ascent. Died of illness during descent.

| 757 | Lena Nielsen-Gammelgaard | Denmark | |
| 758 | Lobsang Jangbu Sherpa | Nepal | |

His 4th ascent. Used no bottled oxygen.

| 759 | Nawang Dorje Sherpa | Nepal | |
| 760 | Tenzing Sherpa | Nepal | |

His 3rd ascent.

| 761 | Tashi Tshering Sherpa | Nepal | |

South Col to Southeast Ridge.
His 3rd ascent.

| 762 | Jon Krakauer | U.S. | 5/10/96 |
| 763 | Andrew Harris | New Zealand | |

Died during descent; cause unknown.

| 764 | Michael Groom | Australia | |

His 2nd ascent.

| 765 | Rob Hall | New Zealand | |

His 5th ascent. Died of exposure during descent.

| 766 | Yasuko Namba | Japan | |

Died of exposure during descent.

| 767 | Douglas Hansen | U.S. | |

Died of exposure during descent.

| 768 | Ang Dorje (Chuldim) Sherpa | Nepal | |

His 4th ascent.

| 769 | Norbu Sherpa | Nepal | |

South Col to Southeast Ridge.
His 4th ascent.

| 770 | Gau Ming-Ho | Taiwan | 5/10/96 |
| 771 | Nima Gombu Sherpa | Nepal | |

His 3rd ascent.

| 772 | Mingma Tshering Sherpa | Nepal | |

South Col to Southeast Ridge.
His 2nd ascent.

773	Tsewang Smanla	India	5/10/96
774	Tsewang Paljor	India	
775	Dorje Morup	India	

North Col to North Face.
These 3 men died of illness and/or exposure during descent.
Their summit claim has been disputed.

776	Hiroshi Hanada	Japan	5/11/96
777	Eisuka Shigekawa	Japan	
778	Pasang Tshering Sherpa	Nepal	

His 3rd ascent.

| 779 | Pasang Kami Sherpa | Nepal | |

His 3rd ascent.

| 780 | Ang Gyalzen Sherpa | Nepal | |

North Col to North Face.

| 781 | Mamoru Kikuchi | Japan | 5/13/96 |
| 782 | Hirotaka Sugiyama | Japan | |

#	NAME	NATION	DATE
783	Nima Dorje Sherpa	Nepal	
	His 6th ascent.		
784	Chuwang Nima Sherpa	Nepal	
	His 3rd ascent.		
785	Dawa Tshering	Nepal	
	North Col to North Face.		
	His 2nd ascent.		
786	Sange Sherpa	India	5/17/96
	His 2nd ascent.		
787	Hira Ram	India	
788	Tashi Ram	India	
789	Nadra Ram	India	
790	Kusang Sherpa	Nepal	
	North Col to North Face.		
791	Hirotaka Takeyuchi	Japan	5/17/96
792	Pema Tshering Sherpa	Nepal	
793	Na Temba Sherpa	Nepal	
	His 4th ascent.		
794	Sven Gangdal	Norway	5/17/96
795	Olav Ulvund	Norway	
796	Dawa Tashi Sherpa	Nepal	
	His 5th ascent.		
797	Dawa Tshering Sherpa	Nepal	
	His 3rd ascent.		
798	Morten Rostrup	Norway	5/18/96
799	Josef Nezerka	Czech Rep.	
800	Fausto De Stefani	Italy	
801	Gyalbu Sherpa	Nepal	
	North Col to North Face.		
	His 3rd ascent.		
802	Alan Hinkes	U.K.	5/19/96
803	Matthew Dickinson	U.K.	
804	Lhakpa Gelu Sherpa	Nepal	
	His 3rd ascent.		
805	Mingma Dorje Sherpa	Nepal	
806	Phur Gyalzen Sherpa	Nepal	
	North Col to North Face.		
807	Petr Kouznetsov	Russia	5/20/96
808	Valeri Kohanov	Russia	
809	Grigori Semikolenkov	Russia	
	Couloir between North and Northeast Ridge.		
810	Koji Yamazaki	Japan	5/21/96
	North Col to North Face.		
811	Thierry Renard	France	5/23/96
812	Babu Tshering Sherpa	Nepal	
	His 6th ascent. Used no bottled oxygen.		
813	Dawa Sherpa	Nepal	
	South Col to Southeast Ridge.		
814	Ed Viesturs	U.S.	5/23/96
	His 4th ascent. Used no bottled oxygen.		
815	David Breashears	U.S.	
	His 3rd ascent.		

#	NAME	NATION	DATE
816	Robert Schauer	Austria	
	His 2nd ascent.		
817	Jamling Tenzing Norgay	India	
	Son of Tenzing.		
818	Araceli Segarra	Spain	
819	Lhakapa Dorje Sherpa	Nepal	
	His 2nd ascent. Used no bottled oxygen.		
820	Dorje Sherpa	Nepal	
821	Jangbu Sherpa	Nepal	
	His 2nd ascent.		
822	Muktu Lhakpa Sherpa	Nepal	
823	Thilen Sherpa	Nepal	
	South Col to Southeast Ridge.		
824	Jesus Martinez	Spain	5/23/96
	South Pillar to South Col.		
	Used no bottled oxygen.		
825	Ang Rita Sherpa	Nepal	5/23/96
	His 10th ascent. Used no bottled oxygen.		
826	Göran Kropp	Sweden	
	South Pillar to South Col to Southeast Ridge.		
	Under his own power from home to summit.		
	Used no bottled oxygen.		
827	Hans Kammerlander	Italy	5/24/96
	North Col to North Face.		
	23.5 hours, Base Camp to Summit to Base Camp.		
	Used no bottled oxygen. Descended most of the route on skis.		
828	Yuri Contreras	Mexico	5/24/96
829	Hector Ponce de Leon	Mexico	
	North Col to North Face.		
830	Ian Woodall	South Africa & U.K.	5/25/96
831	Cathy O'Dowd	South Africa	
832	Bruce Herrod	U.K.	
	Died during descent.		
833	Pemba Sherpa	Nepal	
834	Ang Dorje Sherpa	Nepal	
835	Lama Jangbu	Nepal	
	South Col to Southeast Ridge.		
836	Clara Sumarwati	Indonesia	9/26/96
837	Kaji Sherpa	Nepal	
	His 4th ascent.		
838	Gyalzen Sherpa	Nepal	
839	Ang Gyalzen Sherpa	Nepal	
	His 2nd ascent.		
840	Dawa Tshering Sherpa	Nepal	
	His 3rd ascent.		
841	Chuwang Nima Sherpa	Nepal	
	North Col to North Face		
	His 4th ascent.		
842	Choi Jong-Tai	South Korea	10/11/96
843	Shin Kwang-Chal	South Korea	
844	Paneru Sherpa	Nepal	
	His 4th ascent.		

#	NAME	NATION	DATE
845	Keepa Sherpa (Kipa)	Nepal	
	His 2nd ascent.		
846	Dawan Tamang	Nepal	
	South Col to Southeast Ridge.		
	His 2nd ascent.		
872	Björn Olafsson	Iceland	5/21/97
873	Hallgrimur Magnusson	Iceland	
874	Einar Stefansson	Iceland	
	South Col to Southeast Ridge.		
898	Tashi Tenzing	Australia	5/23/97
	First grandson of any summiteer.		
899	Veikka Gustafsson	Finland	
	South Col to Southeast Ridge.		
	His 2nd ascent. Used no bottled oxygen.		
932	Kai Zhong	China	5/29/97
	North Col to North Face. His 2nd ascent.		

Acknowledgments

Göran Kropp

SPONSORS

Ericsson Mobile Communication
Svenska Dagbladet
Bola
Crux
Energizer
Friluftsfrämjandet
Fuji
Haglöfs
Hestra Handsken
IBM

IDG Europe
Monark Crescent
Pack Track
Pakistan International Airlines
Primus
Salomon
Sparbanken Finans
Sätila
Texet
Öhrling Coopers & Lybrand

LOCAL SPONSORS

Elmia
Holmgrens Bil
Jönköpings Energi
Jönköpings Kommun
Jönköpings Posten
Konradsson Kakel
ROL Inredningar

Saab Combitech
Sparbanken Huskvarna
Svenska Budskap
Teleproffs
Trailergruppen
TV4 Jönköping/Borås
Vätterhem

ALL OTHERS (in random order)

My parents: Sigrun Hellmansson—because you let me go, and Gerard Kropp—for your interest; Grandma Mary Kropp; my accountant Thorbjörn Johansson—for the help with my finances at Gain AB; Magnus Roman—for all pictures and footage; Fredrik Blomqvist—for all footage and pictures; Anna Casel—for letting Fredrik come with me; Jaroslav Chlumsky; Renata Chlumska—for your love; Wongchu Sherpa and Mahadev; Ang Rita Sherpa; Kami Sherpa; Pemba Sherpa; Staffan Skott; the Cohen family; Hans Einarsson—for help from above; Magnus Nilsson—for the maps; Per Calleberg; Smålands Klätterklubb; Johan Holmgren; Bogi Palfay; Ola Hillberg—for the inspiration; Gunder Höög; Mr. Ulf—one day. . .; Maj-Lis—for taking care of my plants; all climbers on the mountain that season; Lars Cronlund; Sade—for the music.

Alpist Reklam—for the printing; Avocet; the Paratroops—for the good food; Informedia—for the press contacts; Peak Promotion—for organizing things in Nepal; Radio P4; Saab—for the flight and for making great cars; the Swedish Embassies in Tehran, Islamabad, and New Delhi, and the Consulate in Kathmandu; and the consulate in St. Petersburg—for your commitment; Vagnhärad Coffee Shop—for the coffee; Viking Line—for a princely return trip from Finland; IMAX—for all the nice moments on the mountain; the Taiwanese expedition; Mälarö Brygga and Stefan Gård—for the logotype; Trelleborg-Rostock ferry line—my first transportation cheating.

And to everybody I forgot to mention but who's been there all the same. To all of you who did not have faith in me—and there were many of you—it gave me strength!

To all those who sent letters and faxes—thank you, it warmed my heart, and to all those who bought the T-shirts—all the proceeds will go to new adventures!

My publisher, Albert Bonnier—who met me at Yttersta Tvärgränd when I returned.

My editor, Annica Starfalk.

David Lagercrantz

The description of Göran Kropp's childhood and youth, his early expeditions, the trip through Europe and Asia, and the climb of Mount Everest are based on three main sources: long recorded interviews with Göran, his detailed journal, and his video footage (mainly filmed by Fredrik Blomqvist).

Interviews with Renata Chlumska, Magnus Roman, and Fredrik Blomqvist have made the picture more complete.

The descriptions of the people in Base Camp and the disaster of May 10 and 11, 1996, are based on—apart from the sources above—articles in *Esquire*; *Time*; *Newsweek*; *Life*; *Vanity Fair*; *People*; the *Philadelphia Inquirer*; the *Independent* (IN); the *Sunday Times* (Johannesburg); the *Seattle Times*; the *Daily Telegraph*; *Bipuk Guardian*; the *Los Angeles Times*; the *Seattle Post-Intelligencer*; *Sports Weekend*; and *Climbing* Magazine. On the Internet, Nova Online, the IMAX Web site, and Outside Online have provided valuable information. Finally, I am deeply indebted to Jon Krakauer, whose brilliant book *Into Thin Air: A Personal Account of the Mount Everest Disaster* (New York: Anchor Books, 1997) is a source from which I have borrowed liberally.

David Asarnoj has done an excellent job finding material in databases.
The journalist Elizabeth Hawley has furnished statistical information.
Malin Lundberg has made linguistic improvements.
Annica Starfalk has scrutinized the text, checked facts, and made the text sharper and more concise in a number of places.
The climber Magnus Nilsson made wonderful maps.
Thanks to Janne Kotschack, for introducing me to Göran.
Thanks to Annika Persson and Abbe Bonnier, for giving me the opportunity to write the book.
Thanks to Göran and Renata, for your warmth and generosity.
Thanks to everybody at Bokförlaget DN, my Swedish publisher, for your endless good humor.
Thanks to John Eyre, for your talent in graphic design.
Thanks to my family, for putting up with me during the summer of 1997 when I wrote the book.
Thanks, little Signe, for interrupting me so often; and Malin, I'm sorry I was so hopeless.

SWEDISH-TO-ENGLISH TRANSLATOR
Ola Klingberg

AMERICAN EDITOR
Ed Webster, publications director, American Alpine Club

WRITERS' ADDITIONAL SOURCES

Jim Curran, *K2: Triumph and Tragedy* (Seven Oaks, England: Hodder & Stoughton, 1987).

Claudia Glenn Dowling, "Death on the Mountain," *Life* (August 1996).

Everest Archives, Royal Geographic Society, London.

Peter Gillman, ed., *Everest—The Best Writing and Pictures from Seventy Years of Human Endeavor* (Boston: Little, Brown, 1993).

Edmund Hillary, *High Adventure* (London: Hodder & Stoughton, 1955).

John Hunt, *The Ascent of Everest* (London: Hodder & Stoughton, 1954).

Reinhold Messner, *Everest: Expedition to the Ultimate* (London: Kaye & Ward, 1979) and *The Crystal Horizon* (Wiltshire, England: Crowood Press, 1989).

Walt Unsworth, *Everest* (Sparkford, England: Oxford University Press, 1989).

Index

About the Authors

GÖRAN KROPP first climbed a mountain at age six, but did not develop a passion for the sport until joining the military after high school. With single-minded pursuit, he devoted his life to training and the quest for mountain conquests. In 1993, Kropp became the second person to reach the summit of K2, the second-highest mountain in the world, without supplemental oxygen. He followed his record-breaking feat chronicled here with a May 1999 cleanup project on Everest, in which he collected empty oxygen bottles and other debris piled there, and summitted once again. For his next adventure, he plans to sail from Sweden to the Antarctic and ski to the South Pole.

DAVID LAGERCRANTZ is a freelance journalist in Sweden.